Things That Kings Can't Do

Other Works by Al Hill

O Come, Let God Adore Us
And Other Sermons for Advent and Christmas

Not Exactly What They Expected
And Other Sermons for Holy Week and Easter

Our Evil—God's Good
And Other Sermons from Genesis through Joshua

In the Presence of the Lord
And Other Sermons from the Psalms and the Prophets

Walking with Jesus
And Other Sermons from the Gospel of Matthew

God's Purpose for Your Faith
And Other Sermons from the Gospel of Mark, Hebrews, James and 1st Peter

From Jerusalem to Jericho
And Other Sermons from the Gospel of Luke and the Acts of the Apostles

Traits of the Shepherd
And Other Sermons from the Gospel of John, 1st John and Revelation

Making Peace with Your Father
And Other Sermons from Paul's Letters to the Romans and Corinthians

The Empty God
And Other Sermons from the Shorter Letters of Paul

DEAR TRINITY
Letters from a Pastor to His People

Things That Kings Can't Do

*And Other Sermons
from Judges through 2nd Kings, and the Wisdom Books*

Al Hill

SOMMERTON
HOUSE

Copyright © 2018 Al Hill

All rights reserved. No part of this book may be used or reproduced by any means, graphic, electronic, or mechanical, including photocopying, recording, taping or by any information storage retrieval system without the written permission of the author except in the case of brief quotations embedded in critical articles and reviews.

Scripture quotations marked "KJV" are from the King James Version of the Bible.

Scripture quotations marked "RSV" are from the Revised Standard Version of the Bible, copyright © 1946, 1952 and 1971, by the National Council of the Churches of Christ in the United States of America. Used by permission. All rights reserved.

Scripture quotations marked "TLB" are taken from The Living Bible copyright © 1971. Used by permission of Tyndale House Publishers, Inc., Carol Stream, Illinois 60188. All rights reserved.

Scripture quotations marked "NIV" are from the Holy Bible, New International Version®, NIV®, copyright © 1973, 1978, 1984 and 2011, by Biblica, Inc.™ Used by permission of Zondervan. All rights reserved worldwide.

Scripture quotations marked "NRSV" are from the New Revised Standard Bible, copyright © 1989, by the National Council of the Churches of Christ in the United States of America. Used by permission. All rights reserved.

Scripture quotations marked "NLT" are taken from the Holy Bible, New Living Translation, copyright ©1996, 2004 2015, by Tyndale House Foundation. Used by permission of Tyndale House Publishers, Inc., Carol Stream, Illinois 60188. All rights reserved.

Scripture quotations marked "ESV" are from the ESV® Bible (The Holy Bible, English Standard Version®), copyright © 2001, by Crossway, a publishing ministry of Good News Publishers. Used by permission. All rights reserved.

Scripture quotations marked "CSB" are taken from the Christian Standard Bible®, Copyright © 2017, by Holman Bible Publishers. Used by permission. Christian Standard Bible®, and CSB® are federally registered trademarks of Holman Bible Publishers.

Cover design by the author.
Cover image © Adobe Stock.

The cover image of the Syrian general Naaman dipping himself in the Jordan River to cure his leprosy (as directed by the Prophet Elisha) is part of a stained-glass window located in St Mary Abbot's Church on Kensington High Street in London, UK. The image is used with the kind permission of the church's vicar, the Reverend Prebendary Gillean Craig, and churchwardens Hannah Stewart and Jamie Dunford Wood.

ISBN: 978-1-948773-12-6 (sc)

Library of Congress Control Number: 2018903541

To learn more about or purchase this or other works by Al Hill,

go to www.sommertonhouse.com,

or www.amazon.com/author/alhill.

Dedication

To Jeff Stinson and Frank Samuels—
the pastors of my childhood and youth, respectively.

I had no idea how hard their job was—
or how well they did it—
until I tried to do that job myself.
And though I am very different from them
in temperament, personality and perspective,
I did my best work as a pastor
when I did what I had seen them do.

Contents

Dedication v
Preface ix

Sermons

From the Book of Judges
Chapter 1. **Lesser Gods—Easier Ways** 5
Chapter 2. **Prove It!** 13
Chapter 3. **Blinded by Strength** 21

From the First Book of Samuel
Chapter 4. **Let a Mother Pray** 31
Chapter 5. **If He Calls You** 39
Chapter 6. **Inauguration Day** 47
Chapter 7. **A Fool by Any Other Name** 59

From the Second Book of Samuel
Chapter 8. **They Could Not Keep Him Out** 67
Chapter 9. **David's House** 77
Chapter 10. **The Forever House** 85
Chapter 11. **Hope in the Darkness** 93
Chapter 12. **Love is Not Enough** 103
Chapter 13. **Sing to God** 113

From the First Book of Kings
Chapter 14. **What Shall God Give You?** 121
Chapter 15. **In the House of the Lord** 131
Chapter 16. **God's Food in the Desert** 141

From the Second Book of Kings
Chapter 17. **Things That Kings Can't Do** 151
Chapter 18. **Holy Housecleaning** 159

From the Book of Esther
Chapter 19. **For Such a Time as This** 169

From the Book of Job
Chapter 20. **Who Died and Made You God?** 179
Chapter 21. **Is That Your Final Answer?** 187

From the Book of Proverbs
Chapter 22. **The Wisest Thing You'll Ever Do** 195
Chapter 23. **A Word To (and From) the Wise** 203

From the Book of Ecclesiastes
Chapter 24. **Is That All There Is?** 215

Indices

Sermon Titles in Alphabetical Order 225
Sermon Texts in Biblical Order 226
Sermon Texts in Lectionary Order 229
Additional Scriptures Referenced 232
Related Sermons in Other Volumes 240

Preface

We live in a remarkable time.

Never in the history of the world has the human race amassed so much power and wisdom (or, at least, knowledge). The great nations of our day make ancient empires seem puny by comparison. They—and a growing number of the world's relatively insignificant states—now have the power to destroy large portions of the globe and its population. The amount of information available about everything is now infinitely greater than ever before, and infinitely more accessible to anyone anywhere who possesses, or can get to, a computer, TV or telephone. And these realities have not reached their zenith; they keep expanding exponentially.

In this modern age of marvels, our power provides prosperity for many—and yet, imperils everyone. Our knowledge makes us well-informed, but it does not make us wise. We use—and abuse—everything.

We have power and knowledge, but regardless of all we have—and will have in the days and years to come—there will always be things that very powerful people can't do (because they are not *all-*powerful). There are, and will always be, limits on the "towers" the brilliant, but not all-knowing, can build.[1]

---

[1] Genesis 11:1-9.

And in this fundamental way, we are just like the primitive people we read about in the ancient texts of Hebrew scripture. In the pages of the Bible, power is a gift given by God as grace, but it may evaporate like a morning mist when taken for granted or turned to ungodly purposes. Wisdom does not come as the culmination of human discovery. It is revealed in response to a counter-intuitive commitment to divine guidance.

Whatever you think or have been told, you cannot "have it all." You cannot do it all. You cannot know it all.

But you can know God, and His will for your life. You can do His will (with His help) and have a relationship with Him that conveys great power. And you can learn how this is possible as you look at key figures in the history of Israel and consider the wisdom God provided His people in this crucial time.

In the pages that follow, there are sermons drawn from the early days of Israel as a people living (often problematically) in the land their God had promised and provided them. There are sermons from the early days of Israel becoming a nation-state, with the individuals and families who were key in God's ongoing plan for His people. And there are sermons from Israel's long tradition of reflecting on what it meant to be God's special people.

Some explanation of process may be appropriate and helpful at this point. All the sermons in this book were written in full manuscript and formatted for preaching to a congregation in worship. Reading them privately as opposed to hearing them publicly will necessarily produce a different experience. But what you lose by not having facial expressions, gestures, tone and inflexion to augment the presentation may be offset by your ability to re-read, pause for consideration, pick the specific sermon you want to "receive," and avoid the natural distractions a room full of people can generate at critical moments in a presentation.

As with previous volumes, I have attempted to provide the full text(s) of every sermon in the version that was used to prepare it. Copyright restrictions make it impossible to do this in every instance. In a few instances, one copy of a passage has been made to serve for more than one sermon. When two scripture readings were included in the worship service (which was frequently the case), it was not uncommon for the sermon to draw themes and insights from both. And when that was the case, both passages have been provided before the sermon.

You will find that nouns and pronouns referring to the Father, Son, and Holy Spirit have been capitalized in the bodies of the sermons, despite the current convention to do otherwise. The same references to God in copyrighted scripture passages are, however, rendered as published.

I have also tried to make this collection useful to those who prepare sermons, by adding footnotes (that were not included in the oral delivery of the sermons), and indices that provide orderly access to titles, texts, lectionary uses and mentions of verses within the bodies of the sermons. It should be noted that the preaching schedule followed the Revised Common Lectionary some years, but not all. As a result, not all sermon texts will be found in the Lectionary Readings index—and two sermons are based on the same text.

Sermons

From the Book of Judges

Judges 2:7, 10-14 ESV

⁷ And the people served the LORD all the days of Joshua, and all the days of the elders who outlived Joshua, who had seen all the great work that the LORD had done for Israel.

¹⁰ And all that generation also were gathered to their fathers. And there arose another generation after them who did not know the LORD or the work that he had done for Israel.

¹¹ And the people of Israel did what was evil in the sight of the LORD and served the Baals. ¹² And they abandoned the LORD, the God of their fathers, who had brought them out of the land of Egypt. They went after other gods, from among the gods of the peoples who were around them, and bowed down to them. And they provoked the LORD to anger. ¹³ They abandoned the LORD and served the Baals and the Ashtaroth. ¹⁴ So the anger of the LORD was kindled against Israel, and he gave them over to plunderers, who plundered them. And he sold them into the hand of their surrounding enemies, so that they could no longer withstand their enemies.

Matthew 7:13-19 ESV

[Jesus said:]

¹³ "Enter by the narrow gate. For the gate is wide and the way is easy that leads to destruction, and those who enter by it are many. ¹⁴ For the gate is narrow and the way is hard that leads to life, and those who find it are few.

¹⁵ "Beware of false prophets, who come to you in sheep's clothing but inwardly are ravenous wolves. ¹⁶ You will recognize them by their fruits. Are grapes gathered from thorn bushes, or figs from thistles? ¹⁷ So, every healthy tree bears good fruit, but the diseased tree bears bad fruit. ¹⁸ A healthy tree cannot bear bad fruit, nor can a diseased tree bear good fruit. ¹⁹ Every tree that does not bear good fruit is cut down and thrown into the fire."

1.

Lesser Gods—Easier Ways

Judges 2:7, 10-14; Matthew 7:13-19 ESV

When they write the history of our time—when they tell what happened in our day, and why—will it sound like something out of the Bible? Will it sound like what we read today?

There was a time when people served the Lord. They had seen what great miracles the Lord had done for them, and their leaders led them to serve the Lord all their days. But when that generation was gone, another followed that did not know the Lord—that had not seen what the Lord had done for them.

And, in time, those people who did not know the Lord abandoned Him, and went after other, lesser gods. And centuries later, when the history of their time was written, it was told as tragedy, because the consequences of their faithlessness to their Lord led inevitably to their destruction.

If our time is like the time of the Judges, when a faithful generation gave way to a rebellious one, we should not be surprised to see God giving us over to plunderers and selling us into the hands of our enemies. It is as though the Lord were saying, "Let the gods you worship watch out for you. Let the gods you serve sustain you. Let the gods to whom you have given yourselves, give you what you need."

And the tragedy of their time and ours is that those who choose to follow other gods think their chosen gods *can* protect them, and sustain them, and meet their every need—and desire. They are not concerned that the God they have abandoned will abandon them in turn.

☙❧

So who are these lesser gods so many people are so eager to embrace?

In Bible times, they were the gods of the Canaanite neighbors of the children of Israel. When the Israelites left some of the pagan people in place around them, they left their pagan gods in place as well. And the history of that time was that the Canaanites had a far easier time drawing the children of Israel into the worship of *their* gods—like Baal and Ashtoreth—than the Israelites did in converting the Canaanites to the worship of the God of Abraham, Isaac and Jacob.

And why would these lesser gods be so enticing?

Simply put: Worshipping the gods and goddesses of the Canaanites was easier—and more fun. They didn't demand as much of their devotees as Israel's God did of His, in terms of covenant loyalty and moral restraint.

Baal and his consort, Ashtoreth, were just supposed to ensure the fertility of crops, livestock, and people. And worship consisted of "showing them how to do that," and celebrating when they brought the rain, and new life to family, flock and field.

And generation after generation, Israelites would look it all over and decide, "Yea, I think I'll give this Baal worship a go." And off they'd go, down the wide, easy way to destruction. As the old saying goes, "It seemed like a good idea at the time"—time and time again.

And it was still a problem when the historians in the Bible were writing about that time centuries later. They were writing about it to show their own generation that following old Baal and

From Judges 2

Ashtoreth was responsible for every bad thing that had happened to Israel ever since that first new generation took over after Joshua and the faithful elders led the people into the land.

But who wants to learn from the mistakes of the past when you're having so much fun making the same mistakes in the present?

Of course, today, Baal and his girlfriend Ashtoreth don't have the allure they once did. The whole pagan idol thing has gotten a bit old, though when people abandon the Lord, they tend to become suckers for anything—even antique stupidity.

But mostly, we're making the same mistakes differently now. We live in what has become a proudly post-modern world. And with all the technological, economic and psychological advancements that amaze us, our world has also multiplied those things that can qualify as "lesser gods" in our lives.

So if you do not know the Lord—if you do not know what He has done for you—and think the smartest thing you can do is abandon the Lord—Who brought the children of Israel out of bondage (and you out of who knows what kinds of jams you were in) Who created you and everything else and everything necessary to keep you alive and well, in this world and the next—if you do not know the Lord—you might choose any one (or more) of an almost limitless line of lesser gods.

෴

You could choose money to be your god—either because you have it, or because you don't. You can "worship" money either way; it doesn't really matter. If you happen to have a lot of money, you can make a fetish out of spending it or hoarding it. If you don't have much, you can spend all your time and thought on how "wrong" that fact is, and how wronged you have been by whoever or whatever stands in the way of your desired affluence.

Many among our younger generation have made fame their god, worshipping at the altar of the remarkable ability now available to put your picture before the public and publish your every thought or movement for all the world to read.

The freedom to do whatever you desire has become, for a growing number of people, the deity before which they bow. Technology has removed the restraint of undesired consequences from many formerly forbidden activities, and at the same time, expanded the opportunities to engage in them. "What I *want* to do" has replaced "what I *should* do" as the moral code and religious creed of many who serve the god of personal pleasure with fanatical devotion.

And then there is the god of scientific skepticism and intellectual arrogance—an ironic faith in that it presumes to have proven all faith irrational and absurd. Yet the more its adherents seek to destroy the faith of others with their assaults of logic and cynicism, the more they take on the form of a religious cult themselves.

These are but a few of the many defective deities eagerly awaiting the worship of those determined to follow a false god.

❧

In our sin-marred world, there will always be lesser gods appealing to the people the true God has created and called to be His own. And many will turn away from the Lord to go after these gods, to serve them, to bow down to them. And whether these other gods are ancient or modern, the reason for their appeal is the same: They offer the illusion of an easier way.

Life is hard. Even the best of lives are fully furnished with hardship, frustration, disappointment and sorrow. Henry David Thoreau said, "The mass of men live lives of quiet desperation."[2] And women don't get off any easier.

But we want life to be easier—even think it ought to be easier. And when you start thinking that way, you start looking for "the

---

[2] From *Walden*, Henry David Thoreau, 1854.

easier way." And when some way looks easier, the natural inclination is to turn off the hard road onto the easy one.

And there's "the rub."

There is no easier way—not to the place you want to go. Every way that seems easier—that promises to be easier—isn't. It's an illusion. It either gets much harder than the way that seemed harder to start with, or it takes off in the wrong direction, and ends up in the worst place of all. And every seemingly easy way has some god or other urging you to come with him on his wide and wonderful way to destruction.

❦

Why is the way to destruction easy and the way to life hard?

I don't know. I wish it were the other way around, but it's not. The gate you want is narrow—even though you want the gate to be wide. The way you want is hard—even though you want the way to be easy. Lesser gods will not get you where you want to go.

But following them *will* get you on God's bad side. The report on the period of the Judges in Israel was that God's people did what was evil in God's sight. They provoked the Lord to anger. And God made what they thought would be the easy way with the other gods very hard, indeed.

How did He do that?

He let them go down the easy road until it went over the cliff. God warned them—and then let them do what they wanted—and reap what they sowed.

Look around. More and more people are heading down the easy way every day. Even those who ought to know better have drunk some lesser god's Kool-Aid and joined the temporarily joyful journey to a destination no one in his right mind would desire.

Jesus said, *"Beware of false prophets, who come to you in sheep's clothing, but inwardly are ravenous wolves."* False prophets "hawking" the ways of lesser gods.

Lesser God's—Easier Ways

Looks good. Sounds good. But it's all an illusion.

The devil told Jesus when he tempted Jesus in the desert: "There is an easier way to get where You want to go. Follow me and I'll lead You to where you can rule the world without going through that crucifixion business."[3]

It was pure delusion, and Jesus saw it for what it was.

Jesus said, "No, thank you" to the devil. To us, He says,

"Take up your cross daily, and follow me."[4]

"He who loses his life for my sake will gain it."[5]

"The way is hard that leads to life, and those who find it are few."[6]

"I am the way, the truth and the life, no one comes to the Father, but by me."[7]

"Enter by the narrow gate."[8]

The hard way is the only way that works in the end.

❧

When they write about us and our time, far in the future, I suspect they will wonder why so many were deceived by the lesser gods of our day—how so many people who possessed such a heritage of faith in the one true God would abandon Him to bet their lives on illusions of an easier way.

The generation that grew up in the shadow of Joshua and the faithful elders—the generation that enjoyed the blessings of the miracles their ancestors observed—could not read the history future generations would write about them or see the terrible consequences that would befall them and their descendants for choosing lesser gods.

Nor can we read our history today.

---

[3] Matthew 4:8-10.
[4] Luke 9:23, NLT.
[5] Matthew 10:39, RSV.
[6] Matthew 7:14, RSV.
[7] John 14:6, RSV.
[8] Matthew 7:13, RSV.

But God has provided us their history so that we will know what will come of our choices in our day. They were warned about lesser gods and easier ways, just as we have been.

Enter by the narrow gate. The way is hard, but it is the only true God's only way to life.

☙❧

Prove It!

Judges 6:11-17 ESV

¹¹ Now the angel of the LORD came and sat under the terebinth at Ophrah, which belonged to Joash the Abiezrite, while his son Gideon was beating out wheat in the winepress to hide it from the Midianites. ¹² And the angel of the LORD appeared to him and said to him, "The LORD is with you, O mighty man of valor." ¹³ And Gideon said to him, "Please, my lord, if the LORD is with us, why then has all this happened to us? And where are all his wonderful deeds that our fathers recounted to us, saying, 'Did not the LORD bring us up from Egypt?' But now the LORD has forsaken us and given us into the hand of Midian." ¹⁴ And the LORD turned to him and said, "Go in this might of yours and save Israel from the hand of Midian; do not I send you?" ¹⁵ And he said to him, "Please, Lord, how can I save Israel? Behold, my clan is the weakest in Manasseh, and I am the least in my father's house." ¹⁶ And the LORD said to him, "But I will be with you, and you shall strike the Midianites as one man." ¹⁷ And he said to him, "If now I have found favor in your eyes, then show me a sign that it is you who speak with me."

John 6:25-30 ESV

²⁵ When they found [Jesus] on the other side of the sea, they said to him, "Rabbi, when did you come here?" ²⁶ Jesus answered them, "Truly, truly, I say to you, you are seeking me, not because you saw signs, but because you ate your fill of the loaves. ²⁷ Do not work for the food that perishes, but for the food that endures to eternal life, which the Son of Man will give to you. For on him God the Father has set his seal." ²⁸ Then they said to him, "What must we do, to be doing the works of God?" ²⁹ Jesus answered them, "This is the work of God, that you believe in him whom he has sent." ³⁰ So they said to him, "Then what sign do you do, that we may see and believe you? What work do you perform?"

2.

Prove It!

Judges 6:11-17; John 6:25-30 ESV

The Bible is the Word of God. Every word of it is divinely inspired. But sometimes we read the Bible so reverently that we miss the fact that, in some places, it is poking fun at, or pulling our leg about, something or someone. Some of the biblical writers, at least, understood that the only way to share God's message effectively, on occasion, was to serve it up with a little sarcasm, or tell a story tongue-in-cheek.

That's how the story of Gideon starts out. Here's a guy who's going to deliver God's people from the invading hordes who burn everybody's crops and steal all their livestock, and the first time you see Gideon, he's hunkered down in a hole in the ground, doing farm work you normally do out in the open, on the *highest* spot of ground around.

And then the angel of the Lord comes and sits down under an oak tree nearby, just to watch him work for a while. At some point, the angel turns off his "cloaking device" and makes himself visible to Gideon and speaks to him. The angel says, *"The Lord is with you, you mighty man of valor!"*—to a man hiding down in a winepress.

Whatever the angel looks like, his appearance leaves Gideon a little less than impressed. And we know this because—however afraid Gideon is of the Midianite raiders—he isn't afraid to shoot right back at this guy (this angel) who has suddenly appeared under the tree: "Well, if God is *with* us, why isn't He doing more *for* us? When is this God I heard so many good things about growing up going to live up to His big reputation in the present?"

Maybe the angel didn't come "in uniform" because Gideon isn't showing him a lot of respect.

☙❧

So God Himself steps in and starts giving orders, "Gideon, go in your might and save your people!" And God must not be making it clear Who *He* is either, because Gideon starts arguing with Him, too.

"Yea, right! Like I could be a hero! I can't do anything. I'm just a peon from Podunk. You don't know what You're talking about."

If you didn't believe in miracles before, you should now, because it must surely be a miracle that, after hearing and seeing such cynicism, God doesn't terminate the conversation—and Gideon—right then.

Instead, God merely says, "*I will be with you,*" which is exactly what the angel told Gideon when he first spoke to him. And because this is one of those things God is always telling people when He comes to see them, Gideon begins to consider that his first reaction might have been a bit hasty and unhelpful, and decides to hedge his bets.

Suppose this "stranger" really is a messenger from heaven or—God forbid!—God Himself! And Gideon starts to backtrack—a little: "If this is one of those divine visitations God is so famous for," he thinks, "and I have found favor with You," he says (though it certainly can't be because of anything Gideon's done or said so far), "then show me a sign that it really is 'You' Who's talking to me," meaning another sign other than the sign God is giving him by coming and talking to him right now in the first place.

From Judges 6

And over the next few chapters in the Book of Judges, as God pushes and prods this remarkably timid "mighty man of valor" into action, Gideon will never stop asking God for more signs, as though "one more sign" is all he needs to know for sure that God is with him and will enable him to do these miraculous things God *may* be telling him to do.

A "mighty man of valor"?

It will take a long time for anyone reading the story to see it. You read about Gideon and want to shake your head in amazement: "How clueless can you get?!" And if the circumstances weren't so dire—and the consequences so tragic—the story would be comic, a farce.

With that in mind, let's modernize the story—and personalize it.

❧

Have you ever thought, when times are hard, and things are tough, and you really are feeling helpless and afraid, "I wish God would just give me a sign," or "I wish God would let me know that He's with me and what He wants me to do," or "Why doesn't God do something about this mess Himself, like He did in the Bible?"

And you hunker down, fully aware of your frailty, your shortcomings, maybe your past failures—waiting—waiting for some special sign to take away all doubt and fear so you can get up and do something.

Fortunately, God is too gracious to say, "How clueless can you get?!"

Even when everybody had gone after other gods, and God let them have their way and suffer all the evil that went with it, He still appeared to His people—in forms they sometimes did not recognize but should have—and encouraged them and guided them and led them to achieve great deeds of deliverance.

Even today, God comes to you and says to you, "Courageous Christian, I am with you!" But "courageous" is the last thing you feel in this world gone mad with anti-Christian venom, and everything you see and hear makes God seem very far away.

"Courageous Christian!"

Does God know something about you that you do not know about yourself—or you knew once and have forgotten?

"I am with you," God says, "even when you are living your life down in a pit. I am with you even when the risks are high, and your suffering has been significant. Go and do the miraculous things I desire you to do. Go and use the power that is in you—the power I placed in you for this purpose. Go because I send you."

"Yes, well, all that may be true. But on the other hand, maybe not. Could you back it up, God, with some indisputable sign, please—something that would remove all doubt?"

But what constitutes "an irrefutable sign"?

Even the Bible says, *"Test the spirits."*[9] You want a sign from God that "settles it." But God rarely gives you that kind of sign.

"Do what I'm telling you to do—be faithful to My Word," God says, "and you will see your 'sign' in the results of your obedience."

God appeared to Gideon and Gideon wanted *another* sign to prove it was really God—and then another and another. Jesus fed thousands of people with almost nothing, and *then* they asked Him for a sign so they could believe in Him.[10] How does that old song go: "If you don't know me by now…"?[11]

Courageous Christian, the sign of God's presence with you is the Person of Jesus Christ, and the bread and wine that are the signs of His Body and Blood sacrificed for you. The sign of the power God has given you is the Resurrection itself—life over death. The sign of God's purpose for you is the fellowship you share as you gather with other Christians around His table and the joy you experience in the service you perform as you reach out in

---

[9] 1 John 4:1, RSV.
[10] Mark 8:1-12.
[11] Kenny Gamble and Leon Huff, "If You Don't Know Me by Now," 1972.

His Name. The sign God gives you is His holy Word that instructs you, and His Holy Spirit that indwells you.

If God gives you more—fine. But if what He has already given you is not enough, I suspect even Gideon will be amazed.

Judges 13:1-5; 16:16-30 ESV

13 ¹ And the people of Israel again did what was evil in the sight of the LORD, so the LORD gave them into the hand of the Philistines for forty years. ² There was a certain man of Zorah, of the tribe of the Danites, whose name was Manoah. And his wife was barren and had no children. ³ And the angel of the LORD appeared to the woman and said to her, "Behold, you are barren and have not borne children, but you shall conceive and bear a son. ⁴ Therefore be careful and drink no wine or strong drink, and eat nothing unclean, ⁵ for behold, you shall conceive and bear a son. No razor shall come upon his head, for the child shall be a Nazirite to God from the womb, and he shall begin to save Israel from the hand of the Philistines."

16 ¹⁶ And when [Delilah] pressed [Samson] hard with her words day after day, and urged him, his soul was vexed to death. ¹⁷ And he told her all his heart, and said to her, "A razor has never come upon my head, for I have been a Nazirite to God from my mother's womb. If my head is shaved, then my strength will leave me, and I shall become weak and be like any other man."

¹⁸ When Delilah saw that he had told her all his heart, she sent and called the lords of the Philistines, saying, "Come up again, for he has told me all his heart." Then the lords of the Philistines came up to her and brought the money in their hands. ¹⁹ She made him sleep on her knees. And she called a man and had him shave off the seven locks of his head. Then she began to torment him, and his strength left him. ²⁰ And she said, "The Philistines are upon you, Samson!" And he awoke from his sleep and said, "I will go out as at other times and shake myself free." But he did not know that the LORD had left him. ²¹ And the Philistines seized him and gouged out his eyes and brought him down to Gaza and bound him with bronze shackles. And he ground at the mill in the prison.

²² But the hair of his head began to grow again after it had been shaved.

²³ Now the lords of the Philistines gathered to offer a great sacrifice to Dagon their god and to rejoice, and they said, "Our god has given Samson our enemy into our hand." ²⁴ And when the people saw him, they praised their god.

For they said, "Our god has given our enemy into our hand, the ravager of our country, who has killed many of us." ²⁵ And when their hearts were merry, they said, "Call Samson, that he may entertain us." So they called Samson out of the prison, and he entertained them. They made him stand between the pillars. ²⁶ And Samson said to the young man who held him by the hand, "Let me feel the pillars on which the house rests, that I may lean against them." ²⁷ Now the house was full of men and women. All the lords of the Philistines were there, and on the roof there were about 3,000 men and women, who looked on while Samson entertained.

²⁸ Then Samson called to the Lord and said, "O Lord God, please remember me and please strengthen me only this once, O God, that I may be avenged on the Philistines for my two eyes." ²⁹ And Samson grasped the two middle pillars on which the house rested, and he leaned his weight against them, his right hand on the one and his left hand on the other. ³⁰ And Samson said, "Let me die with the Philistines." Then he bowed with all his strength, and the house fell upon the lords and upon all the people who were in it. So the dead whom he killed at his death were more than those whom he had killed during his life.

3.

Blinded by Strength

Judges 13:1-5; 16:16-30 ESV

Usually, when the Bible tells you about the birth of a baby—and especially when an angel appears to the parents to tell them that God has seen fit to give them a baby—you expect the kid to grow up into some kind of saint or something. You expect a kid like that to "make his momma proud."

Here's one who didn't: Samson.

Oh, he was supposed to. The angel told his mother he was going to be a Nazarite, a holy man dedicated to God by sacred vows and a sacrificial lifestyle from the day he was born. But something went wrong—terribly wrong—in the case of Samson. Let's see what it was.

Samson was born for a purpose. God gave Samson life and sent him into the world *"to begin the deliverance of Israel from their enemies."* But God, of course, does not assign duties without providing the resources for accomplishing those duties. And so God equipped Samson with superhuman strength. God gave him a gift. And as with every gift of God, Samson's special, spiritual gift—in this case, physical power—was given for a godly purpose.

But Samson didn't "get it."

I think we can assume that his mother and father told him about the angel and the prophecy. I'm sure they explained about the "hair thing" and being a Nazarite. You can imagine how hard they tried to get him excited about what God intended him to do for Israel. But somewhere along the way, Samson started flexing his muscles, and he liked the feeling.

Somewhere along the way, he began to realize he was "special": Nobody else could do what he could do. And, at some point, it also dawned on him that nobody could *stop* him from doing whatever he decided he *wanted* to do. And whatever his parents told him, what he heard was: "Keep the hair—keep the power."

Eventually, he grew his hair so long that it blinded him— spiritually, at least. The way he saw it, his strength was his personal possession—and he began acting accordingly. Samson thought his incredible strength was his personal possession to do with as he pleased—and with it, he could do pretty well *whatever* he pleased. Because of his special abilities, he thought—and acted—as though the rules of God and society didn't apply to him.

❦

But his strength wasn't really his—it didn't belong to him. It was God's. God gave Samson his strength, but it always belonged to God, just like *everything* God gives *all* of us. The strength was a gift, and so was Samson's life. But God didn't give Samson's life just to him; his life was to be God's gift to all Israel. God gave Samson both life and strength, and both were to be used in the way God intended.

Samson enjoyed God's gift. He used it—freely and frivolously—to suit himself. But Samson did not understand God's gift. He did not properly value it or protect it—and so, when he needed it most, he lost it.

"Yes, he lost his strength because he lost his hair."

No, that's not the way it works. You see, Samson's hair was not the *source* of his strength—even if he thought it was. His hair was only the *sign* of his strength. It was a sign of his status as someone in special relationship with the God Who gives great gifts—like uncommon strength.

God was the source of Samson's strength. And so, it was not the loss of hair that cost Samson so dearly, it was the loss of God's Spirit, empowering and protecting him. It seems that the longer his hair got, the more inclined he was to ignore God.

He should have ignored Delilah, instead. Delilah did everything Samson told her would destroy his strength, so, naturally, he ended up telling her exactly what she had to do to "do him in." And surprise! She did exactly that. She shaved off his hair.

But the Bible doesn't say, "He didn't know his hair was gone." It says Samson woke up "and did not know that God's Spirit had left him"—God's Spirit and his strength—because the strength depended on the Spirit. Without God, Samson was nothing and had no power to protect himself from what his enemies—and God's—were all too eager—and now able—to do to him.

❦

The idea of being blinded is awful. But the truth is that Samson was blind long before they put his eyes out, because he had chosen not to see what God had given him life and strength *for*: that from the moment of his conception, and every day of his life, he was under God's providential care *for a reason*.

Then God showed him what it was like to live without that divine protection and provision. The mighty Samson was, without God, just a helpless wretch, lost and blind. But when he finally became helpless—when the mighty Samson had to lean on a little boy—when the blind Samson had to be led by the hand—then God returned to Samson—and returned to Samson the gift of strength, because now the strength would not be Samson's personal plaything, but God's holy power to fulfill the purpose for which God had given it in the first place: to begin the deliverance of His people from the hands of their oppressors.

For the longest time—right up to the end—Samson mishandled his spiritual gift.

But is he the only one?

Paul wrote in Romans that *"we, though many, are one body in Christ, and individually members one of another, having gifts that differ according to the grace given to us."*[12]

Your birth may not have been announced by an angel, but, just like Samson, your life is a gift from God for a purpose God has determined. And you have been given a gift or gifts by God to ensure the success of that purpose. And how easy it is to think the gift belongs to you.

Samson was strong. Perhaps you are athletic or artistic, physically attractive or personally charismatic. Maybe you are blessed with superior intellect, political clout or great wealth. These are wonderful and highly sought-after gifts.

But there is no gift that God cannot take away if you treat it as a personal possession. There is no gift that will long function to your advantage in the absence of God's sustaining Spirit.

The gifts that God has given us are not the source of our success in life, they are the signs of God's presence with us and God's willingness to bless us in the work of the kingdom He has assigned to each of us. God is the Source "from Whom all blessings flow."[13]

Samson went from powerful to pitiful because he devoted his life and God's gift to his own personal agenda. When he would not dedicate himself to the work God created him to do, God finally withdrew His Holy Spirit from Samson.

But here is the good news—the gospel—in the midst of tragedy. After Samson went from powerful to pitiful, he went from pitiful to prayerful, and then from prayerful back to powerful again—but not because his hair grew back. Samson's power returned because the Holy Spirit returned to him. It is a formula

---

[12] Romans 12:5-6, RSV.
[13] "The Doxology," Thomas Ken, 1674.

that works across the board. It's what Jesus was telling His disciples when He told them humility rather than competition for place was the secret to true greatness and leadership.[14]

"*The Lord gives and the Lord takes away.*"[15] The Holy Spirit comes and He goes away as He chooses.[16] And the story of Samson suggests that even when it appears that God has gone away—taken His Spirit away—prayer provides the path for God to send His Spirit back into our lives—with power—to use us and our lives and the gifts He has given us to accomplish the purpose for which He made us to exist.[17]

Samson finally acknowledged his dependence on a Power greater than himself. He acknowledged that whatever power he had was not his personal possession to do with as he pleased. And "seeing" that truth, even in his blindness, he received the greatest power he had ever known—and strength sufficient to do the will of God.[18]

---

[14] Luke 22:24-27.
[15] Job 1:21, CSB.
[16] John 3:8.
[17] Psalm 51:1-4, 7-11.
[18] 2 Corinthians 12:9.

From the Book of 1st Samuel

From 1st Samuel 1 and 3

1 Samuel 1:1-20; 3:19-21 ESV

This is the story of Hannah, a woman who prayed that God would give her a child. God answered her prayer and she gave birth to a son, Samuel, whom she dedicated to the LORD.

❧❦

2 *¹ There was a certain man of Ramathaim-zophim of the hill country of Ephraim whose name was Elkanah the son of Jeroham, son of Elihu, son of Tohu, son of Zuph, an Ephrathite. ² He had two wives. The name of the one was Hannah, and the name of the other, Peninnah. And Peninnah had children, but Hannah had no children.*

³ Now this man used to go up year by year from his city to worship and to sacrifice to the LORD of hosts at Shiloh, where the two sons of Eli, Hophni and Phinehas, were priests of the LORD. ⁴ On the day when Elkanah sacrificed, he would give portions to Peninnah his wife and to all her sons and daughters. ⁵ But to Hannah he gave a double portion, because he loved her, though the LORD had closed her womb. ⁶ And her rival used to provoke her grievously to irritate her, because the LORD had closed her womb. ⁷ So it went on year by year. As often as she went up to the house of the LORD, she used to provoke her. Therefore Hannah wept and would not eat. ⁸ And Elkanah, her husband, said to her, "Hannah, why do you weep? And why do you not eat? And why is your heart sad? Am I not more to you than ten sons?"

⁹ After they had eaten and drunk in Shiloh, Hannah rose. Now Eli the priest was sitting on the seat beside the doorpost of the temple of the LORD. ¹⁰ She was deeply distressed and prayed to the LORD and wept bitterly. ¹¹ And she vowed a vow and said, "O LORD of hosts, if you will indeed look on the affliction of your servant and remember me and not forget your servant, but will give to your servant a son, then I will give him to the LORD all the days of his life, and no razor shall touch his head."

¹² As she continued praying before the LORD, Eli observed her mouth. ¹³ Hannah was speaking in her heart; only her lips moved, and her voice was not heard. Therefore Eli took her to be a drunken woman. ¹⁴ And Eli said to her, "How long will you go on being drunk? Put your wine away from you."

Let a Mother Pray

¹⁵ But Hannah answered, *"*No, my lord, I am a woman troubled in spirit. I have drunk neither wine nor strong drink, but I have been pouring out my soul before the LORD. ¹⁶ Do not regard your servant as a worthless woman, for all along I have been speaking out of my great anxiety and vexation." ¹⁷ Then Eli answered, "Go in peace, and the God of Israel grant your petition that you have made to him." ¹⁸ And she said, *"*Let your servant find favor in your eyes." Then the woman went her way and ate, and her face was no longer sad.

¹⁹ They rose early in the morning and worshiped before the LORD; then they went back to their house at Ramah. And Elkanah knew Hannah his wife, and the LORD remembered her. ²⁰ And in due time Hannah conceived and bore a son, and she called his name Samuel, for she said, *"*I have asked for him from the LORD."

3 ¹⁹ And Samuel grew, and the Lord was with him and let none of his words fall to the ground. ²⁰ And all Israel from Dan to Beersheba knew that Samuel was established as a prophet of the Lord. ²¹ And the Lord appeared again at Shiloh, for the Lord revealed himself to Samuel at Shiloh by the word of the Lord.

4.

Let a Mother Pray

1 Samuel 1:1-20; 3:19-21 ESV

America is broken. The once-great nation is coming apart. We have withstood the attacks of external enemies, but we may not survive our accelerating internal decay. Politicians cannot fix what is wrong with this nation. They don't know how and are afraid to try. Courageous warriors can defend us, but for all their sacrifices, they cannot restore us. The giants of business and industry are dwarfed by the magnitude of the destruction we are seeing. In some cases, they are contributing directly to our demise.

Our only hope may be mothers—mothers who, like Hannah, pour out their souls before the Lord—mothers who ask the Lord for their children and then give them back to God. Today, on Mothers' Day, we honor our mothers—those who deserve honor, who are most of them. And we forgive those few who don't.

But I want to talk specifically—and directly—to those of you who are raising children—or will be—because you are the hope of the future—if there is to be a future in this country. Upon your shoulders—and your lives, your hearts and your minds—lie the responsibility for turning this country around. And Hannah provides the model for what you must do.

Here's the context.

Hannah is a woman—a wife—who lives at a time when her country is in chaos. Israel in Hannah's day is nothing like the great people God called them and led them to be. Israel is up to its eyebrows in enemies. Her tribes have become factions that can neither cooperate nor compromise in the interest of the common good. Hannah is just one woman. She participates in the designated religious activities, but the whole religious system has become empty and sterile—just like her.

There is another woman, Peninnah, who is enjoying life with her kids and taking every opportunity to make Hannah feel miserable about her circumstances. Hannah's husband wants Hannah to be content with his love and the good things he provides her. Even the old priest, Eli, who runs the religious show in Shiloh, doesn't understand her spiritual burden, and gives her grief instead of comfort.

And so Hannah takes her troubles to God. Others are well-meaning or malicious. God is open and able.

Hannah prays. God answers her prayer—and answers the need for renewal in the nation—all at the same time. God gives Hannah a child that she, then, gives back to God. She loves and supports the child even after she has given him to God. And God grows the child into a great spiritual leader of the people, the one God will use to establish the future of the nation for generations beyond Hannah and this child for which she prayed.

And now, let's talk about you.

༒

Over the past 50 years, our culture has slowly and systematically uncoupled itself from its Christian heritage and moral underpinning. You are living through an age when the public consensus about right and wrong has been altered, rapidly and radically. This tragic transformation is nearing completion in the public mind—and even those of us who have opposed the transformation have not been untainted.

From 1ˢᵗ Samuel 1 and 3

Large segments of the Christian community have traded allegiance and given themselves over to the authority of a godless culture. Your neighbors, your friends, your family—all have been influenced, if not completely co-opted. And your children are now targeted for cultural conditioning. If you do not contend for your children, they will not be yours. They will become the obedient children of a value system that rejects you and the God you believe in.

In the Bible story, Peninnah had the children and Hannah had none, and Peninnah delighted in tormenting Hannah about the fact that the children were Peninnah's.

Peninnah is the popular culture. Children will always flock to her—left to their own devices. And she will feed them with generous portions of her "food" and entertain them with worldly resources. And they will become hers.

Hannah went to the Lord and begged Him for her children, and you must do the same. Without God's help, they will not long be yours to love and lead and form into the people they were created to be. They will grow into *her* children—the world's children. And you will be left childless.

Hannah begged God for her child and vowed a vow that, if God would look upon her need and remember her and give her her child, she would give that child back to God. She promised God that *her* child would be *His* child—all the days of that child's life.

ஐ~ஒ

How about you?

What do you think it's going to take for you to be able to raise a child that you and God share, rather than lose that child to the world that respects neither you nor God—nor even the child it has become so adept at luring away from you?

Don't think your child's eternal soul and moral compass will take care of themselves. Don't think your child will be able to refuse the "candy" the world offers, or know to run away from the sweetly-offered invitation to go for "a ride on the wild side," just because you fix the meals and wash the clothes and drive the car to practice.

Mother, you've got to pray—and pray hard! You've got to get tight with God and stay there. You've got to make your life more about what that child will become with God than about any of your own personal goals.

What do you want your child to grow up to be?

If you don't say "God's child!" you've lost that child already.

Hannah poured out her soul to God for her child. She made a solemn promise to God that she would give her child to God. She fulfilled her sacred promise to God by bringing that child to God before the child could even imagine there was an option. Hannah turned her child over to God to be trained in the Word and the work of God, and she continuously and consistently nurtured and supported her child's growth as a servant of God.

And so must you!

Mother, pray for your child—every day. Promise God that you will give Him your child, and *do* that—every day. Train yourself to see your child as God's—a divine gift God has shared with you to bless you as long as you remember the One to Whom the child really belongs. Before you fill your child's eyes and ears with the things of this world, fill them with the sights and sounds of the sacred things of God. Make the people in your child's world people of faith. Seek out other "Hannahs" who are giving their children to God like you are—whose children are also being placed before the Lord continually.

Teach your children the Word of God so that God's Word is part of their earliest and most basic vocabulary. Do not be indifferent to the formation of faith within them. The world will not be indifferent in its effort to eradicate every vestige of faith it finds in them. Foster your child's faith with all the wisdom, energy, persistence and love God gives you. And do not be inattentive to

From 1st Samuel 1 and 3

the insidious influence of the culture that is always in competition with God for the soul of your child.

Peninnah laughed at Hannah and harassed her, every chance she got. The Peninnahs of this world will do the same to you when you resist their efforts to mold *your* children in *their* image. Even well-meaning people will wonder why you're so worked up. Seemingly good people will suggest you just relax and go with the cultural flow.

And if you do, you will be giving your children over to them, and your children will not become the people God created them to be. And they will not grow up to become part of a generation that will turn this nation around—turn it back to God.

Hannah was faithful to the God Who was faithful to her. Here was a mother who prayed and a God Who answered a mother's prayer. She gave God her child.

And what did God do with that child?

God raised him up to speak for God to a people who had lost their ability to hear God. Hannah's child, Samuel, became a man that people knew was in touch with God. And they listened to Samuel. And he led the nation into a new relationship with God.

❦

A generation of children has learned to embrace the culture of drugs and alcohol—and we have filled our prisons and our morgues with them. A generation of children has learned to engage in commitment-less sex and our family structures have disintegrated. A generation of children has learned to obsess over esoteric approaches to "social justice" and ignore the impact of their own personal immorality, and others must now pick up after them or pay to clean up what they have cheerfully destroyed.

A generation of children, nurtured on notions of self-esteem, and the rights both to be happy and to have whatever they want, have not, in fact, grown up at all. Rather, they have put off assuming their proper and necessary roles as adults in favor of an indefinite adolescence spent "esteeming" themselves and seeking that elusive personal happiness our culture has encouraged them to believe they are due by virtue of their mere existence.

These children will not grow up to be what God intended. They will not grow up to fix what is broken, to turn a nation back to the God Who called it into being.

But someone must.

Some mother's child must grow up to know God and hear God and serve God. In fact, many mothers must raise these children in such a way that God can then raise them up to do the work God would have His people do.

Will you be one of these mothers?

Will you be a Hannah to God and your child?

I pray you will.

1 Samuel 3:1-10 ESV

¹ Now the boy Samuel was ministering to the LORD in the presence of Eli. And the word of the LORD was rare in those days; there was no frequent vision.

² At that time Eli, whose eyesight had begun to grow dim so that he could not see, was lying down in his own place. ³ The lamp of God had not yet gone out, and Samuel was lying down in the temple of the LORD, where the ark of God was.

⁴ Then the LORD called Samuel, and he said, "Here I am!" ⁵ and ran to Eli and said, "Here I am, for you called me." But he said, "I did not call; lie down again." So he went and lay down.

⁶ And the LORD called again, "Samuel!" and Samuel arose and went to Eli and said, "Here I am, for you called me." But he said, "I did not call, my son; lie down again." ⁷ Now Samuel did not yet know the LORD, and the word of the LORD had not yet been revealed to him.

⁸ And the LORD called Samuel again the third time. And he arose and went to Eli and said, "Here I am, for you called me." Then Eli perceived that the LORD was calling the boy. ⁹ Therefore Eli said to Samuel, "Go, lie down, and if he calls you, you shall say, 'Speak, LORD, for your servant hears.'" So Samuel went and lay down in his place.

¹⁰ And the LORD came and stood, calling as at other times, "Samuel! Samuel!" And Samuel said, "Speak, for your servant hears."

If He Calls You

Luke 2:41-52 ESV

⁴¹ Now [Jesus'] *parents went to Jerusalem every year at the Feast of the Passover.* ⁴² *And when he was twelve years old, they went up according to custom.* ⁴³ *And when the feast was ended, as they were returning, the boy Jesus stayed behind in Jerusalem. His parents did not know it,* ⁴⁴ *but supposing him to be in the group they went a day's journey, but then they began to search for him among their relatives and acquaintances,* ⁴⁵ *and when they did not find him, they returned to Jerusalem, searching for him.* ⁴⁶ *After three days they found him in the temple, sitting among the teachers, listening to them and asking them questions.* ⁴⁷ *And all who heard him were amazed at his understanding and his answers.* ⁴⁸ *And when his parents saw him, they were astonished. And his mother said to him, "Son, why have you treated us so? Behold, your father and I have been searching for you in great distress."* ⁴⁹ *And he said to them, "Why were you looking for me? Did you not know that I must be in my Father's house?"* ⁵⁰ *And they did not understand the saying that he spoke to them.* ⁵¹ *And he went down with them and came to Nazareth and was submissive to them. And his mother treasured up all these things in her heart.*

⁵² *And Jesus increased in wisdom and in stature and in favor with God and man.*

5.

If He Calls You

1 Samuel 3:1-10; Luke 2:41-52 ESV

Samuel was a good kid—"special" in the way you want kids to be special: respectful, obedient, trustworthy, hard-working. His momma prayed that God would give her a child, and God heard her prayer and gave her Samuel. He was a gift from God, as most kids—maybe all kids—are, really. God gave him to his mother, and a few years later, his mother gave him back to God. Samuel was "a gift that kept on giving."

His momma turned him over to the temple folks before he was old enough to ride a bike—which they didn't have back then. But you get the point.

If you know your child psychology, you can imagine all the kooky hang-ups a kid could develop getting abandoned by his parents like that, so early in life. You wouldn't do what his momma did, at least not until you saw what kind of teenager he was turning into, but by then, of course.... Well, never mind.

But Samuel turned out all right growing up in the old temple there is Shiloh. He got along well with the priest who ran the place. He did what he was told. And when he prayed his "Now I lay me down to sleep..." prayer each night, he did, in fact, go to sleep, contented and at peace.

And then one night, he woke up—or, more accurately, "was awakened." Samuel came out of his sleep because Somebody was calling him—calling him by name.

When you are awakened by some sound in the night, you can wake up disoriented and confused, and Samuel did. But when he finally got it figured out, he found that his whole life was going to change from that night on. And he was, by far, not the only one who was going to "wake up" as a result of what he heard.

❧

Now, at this point, I could go on talking about the story—about Samuel and what he did, and the old priest Eli and what *he* did—and about God and what *He* did. But what I would rather do, is take the story and offer it...as a parable about *you*.

Does that seem far-fetched?

We apply the Bible to our lives all the time. We imagine ourselves sitting in the crowd, listening to Jesus preaching the Sermon on the Mount.[19] We hear Paul talking to the Corinthians about communion and see familiar faces from our own fellowship crowded around the table.[20]

But how do you take the place of young Samuel in the pages of this particular story?

Simple. We just ask Samuel to step aside for a moment while you step in.

You have a number of things in common, if you think about it—if you look at it the right way. Samuel was a gift of God—and so are you. Samuel was given back to God—as you have been—by your own choice, if not that of your parents.

And before some of you start arguing in your mind that *your* momma didn't hand *you* over to some preacher at the ripe old age of three, let me point out that, to God, you are, and always will be, a child—His child—no matter how old you are or get to be. And

---

[19] Matthew 5—7.
[20] 1 Corinthians 11:23-26.

whether your parents brought you to church or not when you were a kid, here you are now, just like Samuel, ministering before the Lord, which is what your worship and other activities in this church really are.

"But I don't sleep at the church!"

Some of you can't say that, of course; I've seen you nod off during a sermon now and then. But, it's true, we lock the place up at night and go home. Nobody spends the night here.

But that does not mean that Samuel is the only one who lies down to sleep in the temple of the Lord. That temple in Shiloh is long gone, of course. So, for that matter, is the one in Jerusalem where Jesus impressed the resident experts when *He* was a boy and perhaps no older that Samuel is here.

But Paul said, *"Don't you know that your body is a temple of the Holy Spirit?"*[21]

Wherever you lie down at night, you lie down, like Samuel, in the temple of the Lord, because the Lord is in you. And more than that, your home is the place where you say your prayers, where you read God's Word, where you break bread in His Name. Do you not suppose that doing that makes it a holy place where God is present?

Jacob went to sleep in the wilderness and woke up in wonder. God had been there where he put his head down for the night—and Jacob didn't know it until he dreamed a dream of a stairway to heaven.[22] And Samuel, for all his time and training in the Shiloh temple, did not know what it meant to lie down in the presence of God until God called him out of his slumber.

Every night, you go to sleep in a sacred place, and every morning, you wake up in the presence of God, whether you know it or not.

---

[21] 1 Corinthians 6:19, CSB.

[22] Genesis 28:10-17.

But, like Samuel, you go to sleep these days amid a darkness that comes from more than the late hour. For Samuel, it was a dark time, night and day, for *"every man did what was right in his own eyes"*[23]—eyes that, from the highest religious leaders on down, had grown too dim to see what God had said was right, morally or spiritually. And because of that, the word of the Lord was rare—visions of the Lord infrequent. And all the people suffered.

"Darkness, night and day" is a pretty fair description of our time. The Word of God—that bright, spiritual torch—is tossed aside gleefully these days as people grope their way into ever darker dangers they define as "finding themselves" and "fulfilling their potential." An army of old "Elis" lead by following, affirming the growing anarchy of our age in the Name of the God they no longer hear or see. This is your world.

But you make your bed in the presence of the Lord. You rest, like Samuel, in a place where "the lamp of God" has not yet gone out.

A part of Samuel's ministry, his service, to the Lord was to make sure that the lamp of the Lord did not go out in the temple of the Lord, the sacred place where he—Samuel—lived. A part of your ministry is to make sure that you tend to the lamp of the Lord that lights your way, to ensure that you do not let the holy light it provides you go out.

If you think the darkness is bad now, imagine how much worse it would be if the light you are responsible for tending went out as well. In that Sermon on the Mount we were listening to, Jesus said, *"If ... the light in you is darkness, how great is the darkness!"*[24]

"But I'm no expert! When it comes to spiritual things, I'm just a 'newbie!'"

---

[23] Judges 21:25, RSV.
[24] Matthew 6:23, RSV.

From 1st Samuel 3

For many of you, that's true. You're like Samuel, new to the process, "young" in the faith (if not so much in years), liking what you see and hear so far, but not sure what to do about all the darkness all around. And that last part is probably true, whether you're "new" at this "church stuff" or not.

And yet, one night, God called the 'newbie"—not the old pro, Eli—but Samuel, the youngster, who didn't know Who it was Who was calling him, or that it could be anybody else other than Eli. Samuel, bless his heart, was clueless. Eli, bless *his* heart, was remarkably slow on the uptake for someone who had spent his whole life as the main guy God was supposedly talking to.

It turns out that God calls anybody He wants to, including you, whether you think you're up to being called by God or not. And God calls *whenever* He wants to, whether you're ready or not.

God called the kid, Samuel. You may be thinking, "Well, I've outgrown that sort of thing." Don't be too hasty. Just remember that God called Moses when he was 80,[25] and Noah sometime *after* his 500th birthday.[26]

Three times, God called Samuel and three times Samuel responded. He got up and "reported for duty"—to Eli. Three times, Samuel interrupted Eli's sleep and, finally, Eli got what was going on.

"If He calls you again...."

୰୶

"If..." Eli says?!

God has been calling Samuel—by name—all night. Do you think He's going to stop before Samuel figures out Who the Caller is and comes running to the right place for a change?

But Eli did clue him in. And this time, God came to where Samuel was and called him.

---

[25] Exodus 3:1-10.
[26] Genesis 6:12-21.

And right where he was, Samuel said what he was supposed to say—what he had been taught to say—what God wanted to hear: "Speak, for Your servant hears."

Yes, Samuel left out the word "Lord" from what Eli told him to say. But now that he knew it was the Lord calling him, and the Lord knew he knew, what Samuel said was good enough for God.

God has given you life and you have given it back to God. You begin and end and spend your day—you live your life—in His presence. You live in His light though the world around you descends deeper and deeper into darkness.

God calls you because you have given yourself to Him. God calls you, ignorant and uncertain as you may be about Him and what He wants—and about what you should say and do in response. And when you don't hear Him, He calls again—and again. And when you hear and don't understand what you're hearing, He calls again—and again.

God calls to you as you rest in His presence. He calls to you—and *for* you—but not just for *you*. He calls you to hear, and He calls you to speak what you hear to those who have gone out into the darkness away from His light. God calls you by name because He knows you and you are His.[27] When you hear Him calling, then *you* know *Him* and that you are His.

If He calls you—*when* He calls you—call Him "Lord," acknowledge your status as His servant, invite Him to speak—and then, hear Him.

"*Speak, Lord, for Your servant is listening.*"

Samuel got it right—finally.

Will you?

---

[27] John 10:2-3, 14-16.

1 Samuel 16:11-13 ESV

Over a thousand years before the birth of Jesus, Israel went from being a loose alliance of 12 tribes to a unified nation with a single king. Because they were the chosen people of God, they believed their king should be chosen by God as well. Samuel, the *religious* leader of Israel, anointed a man named Saul as Israel's first king to signify his divine selection. But when Saul displeased God, God sent Samuel to find and anoint a successor. The person Samuel found was a shepherd boy named David. David was anointed by God's servant and baptized with God's Spirit Who came upon him in power at that anointing.

¹¹ Then Samuel said to Jesse, "Are all your sons here?" And he said, "There remains yet the youngest, but behold, he is keeping the sheep." And Samuel said to Jesse, "Send and get him, for we will not sit down till he comes here." ¹² And he sent and brought him in. Now he was ruddy and had beautiful eyes and was handsome. And the LORD *said, "Arise, anoint him, for this is he." ¹³ Then Samuel took the horn of oil and anointed him in the midst of his brothers. And the Spirit of the* LORD *rushed upon David from that day forward. And Samuel rose up and went to Ramah.*

Inauguration Day

Matthew 3:1-3, 13-17 ESV

Before Jesus began His public ministry, He underwent a public baptism at the hands of John the Baptist, who was already active in Judea. Though John urged people to be baptized as a sign of their repentance of sin, Jesus had no need for such a baptism, and so His was a sign of something else.

¹ *In those days John the Baptist came preaching in the wilderness of Judea,* ² *"Repent, for the kingdom of heaven is at hand."* ³ *For this is he who was spoken of by the prophet Isaiah when he said,*
> *"The voice of one crying in the wilderness:*
> *Prepare the way of the Lord;*
> *make his paths straight.'"*

¹³ *Then Jesus came from Galilee to the Jordan to John, to be baptized by him.* ¹⁴ *John would have prevented him, saying, "I need to be baptized by you, and do you come to me?"* ¹⁵ *But Jesus answered him, "Let it be so now, for thus it is fitting for us to fulfill all righteousness." Then he consented.* ¹⁶ *And when Jesus was baptized, immediately he went up from the water, and behold, the heavens were opened to him, and he saw the Spirit of God descending like a dove and coming to rest on him;* ¹⁷ *and behold, a voice from heaven said, "This is my beloved Son, with whom I am well pleased."*

6.

Inauguration Day

1 Samuel 16:11-13; Matthew 3:1-3, 13-17 ESV

Today is Inauguration Day.[28] The formal festivities of parades and parties will begin tomorrow with a *ceremonial* swearing in of the person who will preside over the government of this nation for the next four years. But, *by law*, according to the Constitution, the official oath of office must actually be sworn today, at noon.[29]

And so shortly after we conclude our worship, one four-year presidential term of office will end, and a new four-year term will begin, with a brief, simple and almost unnoticed event.

The event will be witnessed by a relatively small group of people, and when it is concluded, incredible power and authority will have been bestowed upon one man, and that one man will influence the course of history, for good or ill, until he no longer possesses the power and authority delegated to him—until noon, four years from today, when the *next* presidential inauguration will take place.

As important as today's inauguration will be—and as impressive as tomorrow's inaugural celebrations will seem—we

---

[28] This sermon was preached on January 20, 2013.
[29] U. S. *Constitution*, Article XX (The 20th Amendment), Section 1.

have heard today about two inaugurations that are far more significant.

Three thousand years ago, Samuel sought out a shepherd boy in an insignificant little village and anointed him the future king of Israel. Young David was officially inaugurated for a position whose power and authority would not be provided him unto many years later, when the elders of all the tribes of God's people came to him and publicly asked him to be their king.[30] David began a term in office that day that would last for decades and would establish a dynasty of descendants who would rule in David's stead, not for four years, but for four *hundred* years, and more.[31]

❧

And in Samuel's inauguration of David was sown the seed of another inauguration—the inauguration of a special descendant of David Who would not be born for a thousand years.[32] The inauguration of this Son-of-David-to-come would take place in the waters of the Jordan River at the hands of another well-respected religious leader while a handful (or a hillside-full) of people looked on, without much awareness of what they were witnessing, when Jesus of Nazareth led a very uncomfortable John the Baptist off the bank and into the current that would suffice for the ceremony that started a term in office that will never end.

The baptism of Jesus was His inauguration as the Ruler of the world—the divine and eternal King of kings.[33] That brief, simple, almost-unnoticed ceremony in the Jordan River began a reign that will last for all time[34] and encompass all Creation.[35] It was the

---

[30] 2 Samuel 5:1-5.
[31] 2 Samuel 7:12; 2 Kings 25:6-7, 27-30.
[32] 2 Samuel 7:16.
[33] 1 Timothy 6:15; Revelation 17:14; 19:16.
[34] Revelation 11:15.
[35] Colossians 1:15-16; Revelation 22:5.

inauguration of One to Whom every knee will bow, and of Whose Lordship every tongue will confess.[36]

The baptism of Jesus is a big deal, but like everyone there (with the exception of John the Baptist), we are likely to miss its importance. So let's go back and look again—this time, with the eyes of understanding.

⁂

John the Baptist is baptizing Jews, those Jews who have heard his condemnation of their sins and his call for their repentance.

But *Jews* don't get baptized. Baptism is for people who want to *become* Jews, who want to renounce their former lives and identities in favor of a higher moral and spiritual life as one of God's Chosen people. Baptism is for proselytes converting to Judaism.[37]

But John is calling Jews to repentance just like they were foreigners—filthy sinners—cut off from God—because they are. They preach God's word, but they don't practice it.[38] Nobody does—or can. And some are clear-eyed enough to see that—and courageous enough to admit it—to step forward and say, "My heritage will not make me right with God—my culture will not keep me from suffering the judgment I deserve. I cannot keep God's law. Only God can wash away my sins and all I can do is ask Him to do it."[39]

And there they go, down in the water, praying, "Good Lord, show me the way!"[40]

And then one day, in the midst of all these people who have at least figured out and admitted their problem, Jesus shows up.

---

[36] Philippians 2:10-11.
[37] W. F. Flemington, "Baptism," *Interpreter's Dictionary of the Bible, Volume 1*, New York, NY: Abingdon Press, 1962, p. 348.
[38] Matthew 23:1-3.
[39] See Matthew 18:13.
[40] See "Down in the River to Pray," traditional American spiritual, first published in *Slave Songs of the United States*, 1867, popularized in the movie *O Brother, Where Art Thou*, 2000.

Inauguration Day

Jesus—descendent of King David, born of the Virgin Mary, only-begotten and sinless Son of God the Father[41]—Jesus shows up at John's outdoor revival meeting and says, "Me, too. It's *My* turn to be put under."

And John thinks, "Good Lord, You *are* the Way!" and says as much, though not in so many words.

But Jesus says, "Let's go!" And will not take "No" for an answer.

Jews don't get baptized!

But Jesus is a Jew, and He's going to get baptized.

Well, only *sinful* Jews get baptized.

But Jesus isn't sinful—never has been, never will be, until, of course, God made Him Who knew no sin to *be* sin, for us.[42] But God hasn't done that yet when Jesus comes down to the Jordan. And Jesus plans to get baptized anyway.

John is baptizing sinful Jews who are repenting their sins. But Jesus has nothing to repent of, and still, He demands that John baptize Him.

☙❦

Do you get the sense that *this* is no ordinary baptism? *This* baptism doesn't mean what all the other baptisms mean, just like His crucifixion will not mean what *any* of the other—or *all* the other—crucifixions mean, when they nail His broken body to a cross.

When Jesus goes down in the Jordan River with John—down under the waters flowing over Him like a new grave covering a corpse—His body held there by John's iron grip—it is neither an act of remorse nor a cry of confession. It is, for Jesus, a solemn acceptance of the office to which He has been appointed. It is an

---

[41] Matthew 1:1; Luke 1:26-31; John 3:16; Hebrews 4:15.
[42] 2 Corinthians 5:21.

anointing—an inauguration—of Jesus, as He assumes the position of Savior of the world.[43]

The angels announced His coming and the significance of His birth.[44] The Holy Spirit pointed Him out to the pious in the Temple when He was but days upon the earth.[45] The teachers of the faith were fascinated by Him when He came back to the Temple as a boy, already sensing something of His calling.[46]

But how do You know when the time has come to begin saving the world? Where do You go to get started? How do You begin?

☙❧

Jesus went to the Jordan to be baptized by John. One day, after 30 years of living the life of an average person in an average place—after 30 years, it turns out, of preparation—30 years of potential and promise—Jesus put down the tools of His trade and left the familiar furnishings of home and village, the familiar faces of family and friends—and began a journey to the Jordan that would begin a journey to Calvary that would begin a journey of millions of men and women to heaven.

Jesus began to save the world—and you and me—by doing what those who wanted to be saved were doing, even though He didn't need to be doing it—even though doing what they were doing meant something totally different when Jesus did it.

But that's what Jesus does; that's how He saved—and is still saving—the world. Jesus enters into our lives,[47] foreign to God and filthy with sin though they be,[48] and shares them with us[49] and transforms them into something wholly and wonderfully different

---

[43] John 4:42; 1 John 4:14.
[44] Matthew 1:18-23; Luke 1:26-35; 2:8-12.
[45] Luke 2:22-38.
[46] Luke 2:42-47.
[47] Revelation 3:20.
[48] Isaiah 53:5-6; Romans 3:10, 23.
[49] Hebrews 2:14-15.

Inauguration Day

in the process[50]—just like He did at the Jordan with John and all the "repenters" waiting their turns to wash away their sins.

Jesus went to the Jordan, but He wasn't doing what the rest of them were doing. And because He wasn't, what He *was* doing there would mean that what everybody else was doing would accomplish with God what they wanted to have happen when they went down in the water: *They would be saved.*[51]

Jesus went down in the water—and came up out of the water—and His inaugural festivities really began. The heavens were opened—which means, of course, that the way to God that had been closed was opened. And Jesus saw the Holy Spirit descend on Him, which, of course, is what happened to His ancestor David when he was inaugurated as God's chosen ruler long before—which means that the salvation that had been in preparation for so many centuries was now beginning in the person of Jesus. He had been properly and successfully inaugurated.

And a Voice from heaven said, *"This is My Son, Whom I love; with Him I am well pleased"*—which means the plan of salvation is working perfectly in the person of Jesus.

All this may be true, but even an all-star like John the Baptist was uncomfortable with a process that flew in the face of what he thought God wanted Him to do.

And what did Jesus say to John?

"Let it be so for now; it is proper for us to do this to fulfill all righteousness."

Jesus comes and says, "Immerse Me. Whatever your qualms or discomfort, just do it. It's what needs to happen."

---

[50] John 10:10; 2 Corinthians 5:17-19.
[51] Acts 2:21; 16:31; Romans 5:9-10; Titus 3:5.

But now He's talking to you and what He means is, "Immerse Me"—not in the Jordan or the nearest river you can find—but in your life, in the ebb and flow of your existence—in the dark ground of your consciousness and the deep places of your heart.

"Inaugurate Me" as your Savior, just as the Heavenly Father has done, so that all righteousness—all the things that are right and godly—can be fulfilled—in you—by Me."

To "inaugurate" is "to induct into an office with suitable ceremony." It is "to bring about the beginning of something."[52] Jesus was baptized to inaugurate His reign over us, a reign that would be exercised first by entering into life with us, and then, with His life, transforming ours.

When you watch the inauguration of others, will you not inaugurate Jesus as your God-given Savior and immerse your life in Him as He has immersed His life in you?

---

[52] *Merriam-Webster Dictionary* on-line application, 2017.

From 1ˢᵗ Samuel 25

1 Samuel 25:1-44 ESV

¹ Now Samuel died. And all Israel assembled and mourned for him, and they buried him in his house at Ramah.
Then David rose and went down to the wilderness of Paran. ² And there was a man in Maon whose business was in Carmel. The man was very rich; he had three thousand sheep and a thousand goats. He was shearing his sheep in Carmel. ³ Now the name of the man was Nabal, and the name of his wife Abigail. The woman was discerning and beautiful, but the man was harsh and badly behaved; he was a Calebite. ⁴ David heard in the wilderness that Nabal was shearing his sheep. ⁵ So David sent ten young men. And David said to the young men, "Go up to Carmel, and go to Nabal and greet him in my name. ⁶ And thus you shall greet him: 'Peace be to you, and peace be to your house, and peace be to all that you have. ⁷ I hear that you have shearers. Now your shepherds have been with us, and we did them no harm, and they missed nothing all the time they were in Carmel. ⁸ Ask your young men, and they will tell you. Therefore let my young men find favor in your eyes, for we come on a feast day. Please give whatever you have at hand to your servants and to your son David.'"
⁹ When David's young men came, they said all this to Nabal in the name of David, and then they waited. ¹⁰ And Nabal answered David's servants, "Who is David? Who is the son of Jesse? There are many servants these days who are breaking away from their masters. ¹¹ Shall I take my bread and my water and my meat that I have killed for my shearers and give it to men who come from I do not know where?" ¹² So David's young men turned away and came back and told him all this. ¹³ And David said to his men, "Every man strap on his sword!" And every man of them strapped on his sword. David also strapped on his sword. And about four hundred men went up after David, while two hundred remained with the baggage.
¹⁴ But one of the young men told Abigail, Nabal's wife, "Behold, David sent messengers out of the wilderness to greet our master, and he railed at them. ¹⁵ Yet the men were very good to us, and we suffered no harm, and we did not miss anything when we were in the fields, as long as we went with them. ¹⁶ They were a wall to us both by night and by day, all the while we were with them

keeping the sheep. ¹⁷ *Now therefore know this and consider what you should do, for harm is determined against our master and against all his house, and he is such a worthless man that one cannot speak to him."*

¹⁸ *Then Abigail made haste and took two hundred loaves and two skins of wine and five sheep already prepared and five seahs of parched grain and a hundred clusters of raisins and two hundred cakes of figs, and laid them on donkeys.* ¹⁹ *And she said to her young men, "Go on before me; behold, I come after you." But she did not tell her husband Nabal.* ²⁰ *And as she rode on the donkey and came down under cover of the mountain, behold, David and his men came down toward her, and she met them.* ²¹ *Now David had said, "Surely in vain have I guarded all that this fellow has in the wilderness, so that nothing was missed of all that belonged to him, and he has returned me evil for good.* ²² *God do so to the enemies of David and more also, if by morning I leave so much as one male of all who belong to him."*

²³ *When Abigail saw David, she hurried and got down from the donkey and fell before David on her face and bowed to the ground.* ²⁴ *She fell at his feet and said, "On me alone, my lord, be the guilt. Please let your servant speak in your ears, and hear the words of your servant.* ²⁵ *Let not my lord regard this worthless fellow, Nabal, for as his name is, so is he. Nabal is his name, and folly is with him. But I your servant did not see the young men of my lord, whom you sent.* ²⁶ *Now then, my lord, as the* LORD *lives, and as your soul lives, because the* LORD *has restrained you from bloodguilt and from saving with your own hand, now then let your enemies and those who seek to do evil to my lord be as Nabal.*

²⁷ *"And now let this present that your servant has brought to my lord be given to the young men who follow my lord.* ²⁸ *Please forgive the trespass of your servant. For the* LORD *will certainly make my lord a sure house, because my lord is fighting the battles of the* LORD, *and evil shall not be found in you so long as you live.* ²⁹ *If men rise up to pursue you and to seek your life, the life of my lord shall be bound in the bundle of the living in the care of the* LORD *your God. And the lives of your enemies he shall sling out as from the hollow of a sling.* ³⁰ *And when the* LORD *has done to my lord according to all the good that he has spoken concerning you and has appointed you prince over Israel,* ³¹ *my lord shall have no cause of grief or pangs of conscience for having shed*

From 1ˢᵗ Samuel 25

blood without cause or for my lord working salvation himself. And when the LORD has dealt well with my lord, then remember your servant."

³² And David said to Abigail, "Blessed be the LORD, the God of Israel, who sent you this day to meet me! ³³ Blessed be your discretion, and blessed be you, who have kept me this day from bloodguilt and from working salvation with my own hand! ³⁴ For as surely as the LORD, the God of Israel, lives, who has restrained me from hurting you, unless you had hurried and come to meet me, truly by morning there had not been left to Nabal so much as one male."
³⁵ Then David received from her hand what she had brought him. And he said to her, "Go up in peace to your house. See, I have obeyed your voice, and I have granted your petition."

³⁶ And Abigail came to Nabal, and behold, he was holding a feast in his house, like the feast of a king. And Nabal's heart was merry within him, for he was very drunk. So she told him nothing at all until the morning light. ³⁷ In the morning, when the wine had gone out of Nabal, his wife told him these things, and his heart died within him, and he became as a stone. ³⁸ And about ten days later the LORD struck Nabal, and he died.

³⁹ When David heard that Nabal was dead, he said, "Blessed be the LORD who has avenged the insult I received at the hand of Nabal, and has kept back his servant from wrongdoing. The LORD has returned the evil of Nabal on his own head." Then David sent and spoke to Abigail, to take her as his wife. ⁴⁰ When the servants of David came to Abigail at Carmel, they said to her, "David has sent us to you to take you to him as his wife." ⁴¹ And she rose and bowed with her face to the ground and said, "Behold, your handmaid is a servant to wash the feet of the servants of my lord." ⁴² And Abigail hurried and rose and mounted a donkey, and her five young women attended her. She followed the messengers of David and became his wife.

⁴³ David also took Ahinoam of Jezreel, and both of them became his wives. ⁴⁴ Saul had given Michal his daughter, David's wife, to Palti the son of Laish, who was of Gallim.

A Fool by Any Other Name

Luke 12:13-21 ESV

[13] *Someone in the crowd said to [Jesus], "Teacher, tell my brother to divide the inheritance with me."* [14] *But he said to him, "Man, who made me a judge or arbitrator over you?"* [15] *And he said to them, "Take care, and be on your guard against all covetousness, for one's life does not consist in the abundance of his possessions."* [16] *And he told them a parable, saying, "The land of a rich man produced plentifully,* [17] *and he thought to himself, 'What shall I do, for I have nowhere to store my crops?'* [18] *And he said, 'I will do this: I will tear down my barns and build larger ones, and there I will store all my grain and my goods.* [19] *And I will say to my soul, "Soul, you have ample goods laid up for many years; relax, eat, drink, be merry."* [20] *But God said to him, 'Fool! This night your soul is required of you, and the things you have prepared, whose will they be?'* [21] *So is the one who lays up treasure for himself and is not rich toward God."*

7.

A Fool by Any Other Name

1 Samuel 25:1-44; Luke 12:13-21 ESV

When we read the Old Testament passage today about Nabal and Abigail and David, we left a lot out. It's a long story and we didn't have time to read every verse in the whole chapter. Even if we had, there would still be a lot left out—or, at least, a lot left unsaid.

David's encounter with Nabal and Abigail is a key stepping stone to power for David on his way to becoming king. It also reveals, for the first time, the dark side of this one-time shepherd boy—aspects of his personality that will haunt him, his family and his kingdom throughout his reign, and hinder him from becoming the even greater king that God intended him to be.

But the story begins with someone else. Notice how the Bible introduces him. Before you get his name, you get his financial statement: There was a man who was rich—very rich—so rich that his business interests spread well beyond where he lived. The Bible eventually gives his name as "Nabal."

But that can't be true—not literally. That wouldn't be the name on his birth certificate. "Nabal" is the Hebrew word for "fool."

What parent is going to call his kid "Fool"—officially—on the day he's born?

But that's what he's called in the Bible. And the writer says the name fits his character: He's harsh and badly behaved, for all his wealth and prominence. His servants call him "worthless"—and not just in private. His wife publicly acknowledges that the name fits the man.

How foolish is he?

He's about to get every one of the many men who work for him, and every man in his family, and himself, killed. He's decided his "stuff" is more important than the people who helped him get it and now look after it. There is dumb and there is dumber—and our buddy Nabal is both.

Yes, David is running a protection racket. His "request" for *"whatever you have at hand"* is extortion, no matter how diplomatic and deferential sounding the words are that he uses to package it.

Nabal didn't hire David to protect his business. He doesn't owe David anything. He's well within his rights to refuse to give David and his army of malcontents and mercenaries anything.

But who's going to defend those rights—and his people—when Nabal can't? And even more importantly, did God give him all he has with no expectation that he share it with those who need it—even those who don't deserve it?

Yes, Nabal is a fool.

But is he a fool because he is rich?

No, he is a fool because he is greedy and selfish—and prideful.

❧❧

It is interesting how much he sounds like another wealthy landowner—the probably fictitious farmer Jesus tells about in the parable today.

Jesus obviously knows the story of Nabal by heart, because He seems to be comparing fools when He has the fellow in His parable ask himself, "What am I going to do with so much more than I need?" and then has him decide to put it all in newly built barns instead of the hands of his needy neighbors.

From 1ˢᵗ Samuel 25

Both Nabal and the fool in the parable lose everything their grubby little hands have grabbed up in the course of their greedy lives. They die without warning and—in that instant—everything they think they possess is lost to them, along with their lives. And both men are revealed for the fools they've been.

༺༻

But Nabal isn't the only fool in the Old Testament story we read today. Nabal's greed has made him a fool. And David's anger may make him one, too.

In the chapter before this, and again in the chapter after, David dodges King Saul who has brought a posse down to catch David. Each time, David has the chance to kill the king who wants to kill him—the king who stands in the way of David becoming king himself. And each time, David has enough sense to let Saul live so David can convincingly proclaim himself still a loyal and obedient servant of the king.

But David has an army of his own to feed, and no time or inclination to till the fields and tend the herds—if he had had any—with Saul playing hide-and-seek with him all over the Judean hill country. So he's left to put the pinch on the law-abiding citizens of surrounding towns.

As gangsters go, David comes down on the more civilized end of the spectrum. He doesn't steal Nabal's livestock outright. He hasn't harassed the herdsmen. David asks politely for what he wants—though he means to have it, regardless.

But when Nabal goes to that place in his heart where fools go, and decides to reject David's velvet-voiced demands, and spits out ugly insults in reply, David goes to the place fools go in his own heart.

David decides in his rage and offended pride to wipe out all the innocent people he can get his hands on, regardless of what it will do to his reputation as Israel's great and good hero, or his political path to kingship, or his relationship with the Lord Who is his Shepherd.

David demonstrates that anger can make you just as much a fool as greed can. If anything, anger makes a worse fool, because when you've given yourself over to your anger, you get there faster, and want for all the world to hurt somebody. That's not just foolish—that's insane!

But we all have that place in our hearts where we can go to become fools. It may be a larger place for some than for others. But we all have that place. Some will try to bar the door to make it harder to get in. Some leave the door open wide, so they can go there easily and often.

Greed and selfishness are paths to that place. And, certainly, anger is. Fear can take you there, as can jealousy. But pride... Pride is the passenger that always rides along—or drives you there with unwavering resolve.

What are the two fools, Nabal and David, saying on the way to their mutual disaster?

"I'm special! I deserve special treatment—greater respect and empathy than I'm prepared to give others. I should be treated just how I want to be treated. And I should not have to bend my will to the demands or the needs of others. I have a right to what I want. I have a right to keep what is mine and receive what I think I need from others. And if things don't go the way I think they ought to, I'm going to see that somebody—meaning somebody *else*—pays."

Of course, the truly remarkable thing is not that they are thinking these things. Most all of us think these kinds of things sometime or other, consciously or not.

No, we know these two guys are fools because they're saying these things out loud—in front of witnesses—which, as embarrassing and ungodly as their behavior is, at least lets the people around them know what's going on and gives them a chance to try to do something about it.

From 1st Samuel 25

But notice: Nobody on David's side says a word to him about staying calm and reconsidering the wisdom of what he has in mind. They're all joining in the foolishness, strapping on swords and looking forward to sticking perfectly innocent people with them. David does not yet have a Nathan who will look him in the eye and say, "You're a *fool* if you do this!"

And nobody bothers with Nabal. They've learned not to "argue with an idiot."

But there is a servant of this fool who goes to the only person he knows that he's never known to be a fool. The servant goes to a beautiful woman named Abigail. She's Nabal's wife and she's more than beautiful. She knows how to put a stop to the foolishness. If greed breeds foolishness—generosity overcomes it. If rage ramps up to reckless violence and serious stupidity, humble peacemaking undermines the anger and pulls pride down from it pedestal.

Abigail gathers everything edible she can get her hands on and points the gravy train toward Camp David (or, rather, the camp of David), and follows along behind. Fortunately, for all the fools and everybody else concerned, Abigail gets to David before his boys get to Nabal. And her words to David, spoken inches from his ankles, are even more submissive—and certainly more sincere—than the words David had sent by his servants to her husband.

Abigail saves the day—and many lives—and David from his own worst impulses—this time. Nabal will die a fool—but not by David's hand. Abigail will confront her fool of a husband with the truth of what his greed and pride almost cost him, and it will scare him to death. The Bible's verdict is simple: *"The Lord struck him."*

And in the end, guess who gets all Nabal's precious "stuff"?

The fool who let himself get talked out of being a fool. When the dust of Nabal's death settles, David takes Abigail as his wife, and everything else that was Nabal's—his wealth, his prestige as a local leader, his political clout—are transferred to David as well.

If you can control your anger, your selfishness, your jealousy and, most of all, your pride, you can stay out of that place in your heart where people become fools.

But who of us can do that, by ourselves. Nabal couldn't, and it killed him.

David couldn't, either. But then he got help. Someone wise and beautiful came to him and met his needs and made him see reason. And he recognized that she was his salvation—that she had the words of life, when all he could think about was death. She brought him back to sanity when he had lost his mind. And for that, he made her a permanent part of his life from then on.

There is One Who is infinitely more beautiful and infinitely wiser even than Abigail—One Who comes to us in our foolishness and offers us the words of life that will lead us out of the dark places in our hearts and minds where our pride and pain, our anger and our greed would hold us captive and compel us to the greatest folly. There is One Who promises always to be with us to shine a divine light upon our way, so that our name need not be "Nabal"—Fool.

There is a place in your heart where you can go to be a fool. But there is a God Who can fill your heart with His Spirit Who will dwell with you there forever, touching every part of your heart with the power to be the person He created you to be.

Bring Him into your life.

You'd be a fool not to.

From the Book of 2nd Samuel

2 Samuel 5:1-3, 6-7 ESV

¹ Then all the tribes of Israel came to David at Hebron and said, "Behold, we are your bone and flesh. ² In times past, when Saul was king over us, it was you who led out and brought in Israel. And the LORD said to you, 'You shall be shepherd of my people Israel, and you shall be prince over Israel.'" ³ So all the elders of Israel came to the king at Hebron, and King David made a covenant with them at Hebron before the LORD, and they anointed David king over Israel.

⁶ And the king and his men went to Jerusalem against the Jebusites, the inhabitants of the land, who said to David, "You will not come in here, but the blind and the lame will ward you off"—thinking, "David cannot come in here." ⁷ Nevertheless, David took the stronghold of Zion, that is, the city of David.

☙❧

John 12:12-16 ESV

¹² The next day the large crowd that had come to the feast heard that Jesus was coming to Jerusalem. ¹³ So they took branches of palm trees and went out to meet him, crying out, "Hosanna! Blessed is he who comes in the name of the Lord, even the King of Israel!" ¹⁴ And Jesus found a young donkey and sat on it, just as it is written,

> ¹⁵ "Fear not, daughter of Zion;
> behold, your king is coming,
> sitting on a donkey's colt!"

¹⁶ His disciples did not understand these things at first, but when Jesus was glorified, then they remembered that these things had been written about him and had been done to him.

☙❧

8.

They Could Not Keep Him Out

2 Samuel 5:1-3, 6-7; John 12:12-16 ESV

Today, we wave the palms and sing "Hosanna!" to commemorate the Triumphal Entry of Jesus into Jerusalem, the holy city of God. But before you settle in to enjoy the parade, you may want to take another look. The Gospel writers make it sound like "a good time was had by all." Or, at least, that's the way we read it, because that's what it's become for us.

But things aren't always what they seem, especially in the Gospel of John, and a closer look may reveal some significant problems with the pageant about to proceed up the hill.

The word is out that Jesus is coming to Jerusalem. He's been on His way for some time; it's been no secret. Jesus has been making His way very methodically through the Holy Land to arrive at the gates of the holy city amid the multitude of Passover pilgrims. And He's been performing miracles along the way, just to make the journey interesting: a blind man healed here,[53] a dead person raised there.[54] Jesus has made a name for Himself—and they've certainly heard of Him in Jerusalem.

But the people making all the fuss over Jesus as He approaches

---

[53] Mark 10:46-52.
[54] John 11:38-44.

are not the fine citizens of this sacred city. There's no dignified delegation of the City Council or Chamber of Commerce—or even the local Clergy Club—marching out to meet Him. *"The great crowd"* John describes are the "out-of-towners"—other pilgrims. Luke says "the multitude" is *"the multitude of His disciples."*[55] Matthew and Mark talk about *"many,"*[56] and *"most of the crowd"* and *"others"*[57]— leaving the actual count rather vague.

Jesus is left to secure His own transportation, which He does by sending His disciples to commandeer a donkey from the pool of pack animals most villages keep available in the square, specifically for that purpose.[58] Jesus mounts the beast and the scene begins to look for all the world like a royal arrival at the gates. Jesus mounts a donkey, just like King Solomon did[59]—and probably his father David before him—a thousand years before Jesus—to come into their kingdom—and arrive at their throne—in Jerusalem.

The disciples of Jesus, and at least some of the other pilgrims, "strike up the band" (metaphorically speaking). He looks like the King to them. All Jesus needs is for the Official Welcoming Committee to come out of Jerusalem and offer the standard honors that any arriving dignitary is due.

But the committee never comes. They never come out.

❧

So Jesus comes in.

Despite their insult—despite the opposition and hostility that are so obvious in their action (or lack of it)—the good and great citizens of the City of God cannot keep God's Messiah—the coming King—out. He rides right up to the Temple and enters the

---

[55] Luke 19:37-38.
[56] Matthew 21:8-9.
[57] Mark 11:8-9.
[58] J. Duncan M. Derrett, "Law in the New Testament: The Palm Sunday Colt," *Novum Testamentum, Vol. 13, Fasc. 4* (Oct., 1971), pp. 241-258.
[59] 1 Kings 1:32-40.

place where priests and people proclaim the Presence of God to dwell.[60]

But they don't want Jesus there—they who perform their duties there as the holy smoke rises to heaven every day. They don't want Him there—even though He is the Presence of God Who came down from heaven in human form[61] and is now face to face with them. They don't want Jesus there because they sense He's about to turn everything they stand for on its head. He's about to cast everything out of the Temple that they have gladly brought into it,[62] while they try to figure out a politically safe way to throw *Him* out of the Temple[63]—and out of this world.[64]

And they *will* figure it out, of course—in just a few days. They will see to it that this One Who rode into town—borne like a King upon a donkey—propelled by the praise of the pilgrims—will go out, burdened like a criminal under a cross,[65] assaulted by the insults of those who arranged His execution.[66] And they will be so satisfied with themselves and what they've accomplished—or think they have accomplished...

...until they discover that, even when they kill Him, they cannot keep Him out.

☙❧

When King David first came to Jerusalem, to make it his capital—the place where he would rule—his enemies were sure they could keep him out—out of what they considered their impregnable domain.

---

[60] Mark 11:11.
[61] Philippians 2:6-7.
[62] Matthew 21:12-13.
[63] Luke 19:47-48.
[64] Matthew 26:3-5.
[65] John 19:16-18.
[66] Matthew 27:41-43.

"The blind and the lame will ward you off, Davie Boy!" they jeered. "You'll never get to us—never get past our defenses—never come where we are."

And then, in a way, and with a speed, they had never imagined, David was "there" and the city was his. He had overcome all their defenses—and he was their king.

◈

And in the same way, the leaders of a later Jerusalem raised their defenses—they ridiculed the Prince of Peace, the Messiah of God, coming to them—in accordance with the ancient promises[67]—humble and riding on a donkey. If they thought that even the blind and the lame could keep Jesus out of Jerusalem, they were just as mistaken as *their* ancient ancestors were about *His* ancestor, David. Jesus made the blind to see and the lame to walk.[68]

It seemed so simple to ignore Him. And when that didn't work, it seemed as though it would be embarrassingly easy to eliminate Him: Trump up some charges.[69] Manipulate the Roman magistrate.[70] Torture this Jesus to near madness.[71] And then watch His life slowly drain away.[72]

But alive or dead, they could not keep Him out. On Palm Sunday, Jesus came triumphantly through the great open gates of the city. A week later, He came even more triumphantly through the small, locked door of a room of no importance in the city,[73] except that the room was filled with disciples who thought He could not come in—there or anywhere—because He was dead.

Except He did come in.

---

[67] Zechariah 9:9-10.
[68] Matthew 15:30-31.
[69] Mark 14:55-59.
[70] John 19:12-16.
[71] John 19:1-3.
[72] Mark 15:25, 33-37.
[73] John 20:19.

They could not keep Him out—and they didn't try. Jesus, the Teacher from Galilee—Who entered Jerusalem with all the symbolism of a king—*was* a king—*is* a king—is THE King—is *their* King. He is the King no one can keep out.

Oh, there are many who want to—and try to—keep Him out, still.

"I don't believe in Jesus. I don't want any part of Him. Don't bother me with your 'holy hogwash'—your religious rituals and routine. You can't force me to listen and you couldn't convince me if I did. You can't get through to me with Jesus. My defenses are too strong. He's not my King and He's not coming into my life."

And if that's the way you're thinking, you're wrong—simply—dangerously—wrong.

Yes, you can put up your defenses. You can ignore our entreaties and those of the Holy Spirit. You can reject our arguments and those of the Bible. You can put every barrier possible between you and the Jesus Who wants to—and has a right to—rule over you.

Many people do—a lot of them, our own family members and friends. And they hold Him off year after year after year. And that, they can do—*you* can do—because, like the words of Revelation say,[74] Jesus stands at the door and knocks—just knocks, politely—and calls, lovingly. And if you hear His voice and open the door, He will come in to you—and share the goodness of God with you.

And if you do not invite Him in, He will not come in—though He could. Instead, He will wait. He never goes away, though you may think He has. You see, Jesus is patient as well as polite. And He is the King—your King—whether you acknowledge Him or not. Jesus is the King Who has the right to rule over you. And He can afford to be patient because He knows that He *will* reign over you—by your voluntary submission in this life—or without it, in the next.

---

[74] Revelation 3:20.

Paul put it this way: *"...at the Name of Jesus, every knee shall bow, in heaven and on earth and under the earth* (which pretty much covers all the categories available)—*and every tongue shall confess that Jesus Christ is Lord."*[75]

And when will that be?

When you are no longer in a position to keep Him out—and He is no longer willing to let you—and when you are no longer in a position to benefit from letting Him in.

When will that be?

When you go out of this world—as you will one day—or He comes back into it.

John put it this way in the Book of Revelation: *"Then the seventh angel blew his trumpet, and there were loud voices in heaven, saying, 'The kingdom of the world has become the kingdom of our Lord and of His Christ, and He shall reign forever and ever!'"*[76]

Here's the funny thing: *"The kingdom of this world"* has *always* been *"the kingdom of our Lord and of His Christ,"* from the first instant in time when He created it. He has always been the only rightful King of this kingdom in which we are all subjects, whether rebellious ones or faithful. And He will always be the only rightful King of this kingdom, forever and ever, Amen.

※

So, what's the point of pretending otherwise? What's the point of "passing" on His parade? What's the point of putting up the barricades and trying to keep Jesus out of your life when all you're really doing is delaying your inevitable submission and diminishing the joy and wonder that comes with joining the royal procession and making the most of His triumphal entry into your heart—that place where He has the right to rule anyway?

What's the point?

There isn't any point.

---

[75] Philippians 2:10-11, TLB.
[76] Revelation 11:15, RSV.

They could not keep Jesus out of Jerusalem any more than David could be kept out a thousand years before. And you cannot keep Jesus out—nor should you.

You can ignore Him. You can attack Him.

But it won't keep Him from being the King Who will sooner or later rule over everybody everywhere, including you.

❧

And if you make Him your King now?

You get to march in His royal parade. You get to go out to meet Him and welcome Him and usher Him into your life. You get to celebrate His arrival. You get to go to heaven with Him and enjoy His blessings on earth.

And if Revelation is to be believed, you get to sit with Him on His throne in heaven,[77] which, you'll admit, not a lot of other kings would ever let you do.

When the leaders of Israel went to make David their king, they told him, "You led us out and brought us in." They said, "God made you His shepherd over us to rule over us."

And so we say to David's greatest descendant, Jesus: "Be our King. Lead us. Shepherd us. Come and rule over us. You are the King."

❧

---

[77] Revelation 3:21.

David's House

2 Samuel 7:1-16 ESV

David went from shepherd boy to wilderness warlord to king of the children of Israel. And yet, when, as king, David decided to build a house—a temple—for God, God refused David this honor. But God promised David that David's house—his dynasty—would reign forever after him, and that a son of David would build God's temple.

❧

¹ Now when the king lived in his house and the LORD had given him rest from all his surrounding enemies, ² the king said to Nathan the prophet, "See now, I dwell in a house of cedar, but the ark of God dwells in a tent." ³ And Nathan said to the king, "Go, do all that is in your heart, for the LORD is with you."

⁴ But that same night the word of the LORD came to Nathan, ⁵ "Go and tell my servant David, 'Thus says the LORD: "Would you build me a house to dwell in? ⁶ I have not lived in a house since the day I brought up the people of Israel from Egypt to this day, but I have been moving about in a tent for my dwelling. ⁷ In all places where I have moved with all the people of Israel, did I speak a word with any of the judges of Israel, whom I commanded to shepherd my people Israel, saying, 'Why have you not built me a house of cedar?'"'

⁸ "Now, therefore, thus you shall say to my servant David, 'Thus says the LORD of hosts, "I took you from the pasture, from following the sheep, that you should be prince over my people Israel. ⁹ And I have been with you wherever you went and have cut off all your enemies from before you. And I will make for you a great name, like the name of the great ones of the earth. ¹⁰ And I will appoint a place for my people Israel and will plant them, so that they may dwell in their own place and be disturbed no more. And violent men shall afflict them no more, as formerly, ¹¹ from the time that I appointed judges over my people Israel. And I will give you rest from all your enemies. Moreover, the LORD declares to you that the LORD will make you a house. ¹² When your days are fulfilled and you lie down with your fathers, I will raise up your offspring after you, who shall come from your body, and I will establish his

From 2nd Samuel 7

kingdom. [13] He shall build a house for my name, and I will establish the throne of his kingdom forever. [14] I will be to him a father, and he shall be to me a son. When he commits iniquity, I will discipline him with the rod of men, with the stripes of the sons of men, [15] but my steadfast love will not depart from him, as I took it from Saul, whom I put away from before you. [16] And your house and your kingdom shall be made sure forever before me. Your throne shall be established forever.""

Acts 13:22-23, 32-38 ESV

The Apostle Paul and all the early disciples proclaimed Jesus as the descendent of King David Who was the fulfillment of God's promise to David of a descendent who would reign forever. Paul is here preaching to Jews and gentiles alike about the resurrected Jesus Who is the son of David.

❧

[Paul said:]
²² "And when [God] had removed [King Saul], he raised up David to be their king, of whom he testified and said, 'I have found in David the son of Jesse a man after my heart, who will do all my will.' ²³ Of this man's offspring God has brought to Israel a Savior, Jesus, as he promised."

³² "And we bring you the good news that what God promised to the fathers, ³³ this he has fulfilled to us their children by raising Jesus, as also it is written in the second Psalm,

'You are my Son,
today I have begotten you.'

³⁴ And as for the fact that he raised him from the dead, no more to return to corruption, he has spoken in this way,

'I will give you the holy and sure blessings of David.'

³⁵ Therefore he says also in another psalm,

'You will not let your Holy One see corruption.'

³⁶ For David, after he had served the purpose of God in his own generation, fell asleep and was laid with his fathers and saw corruption, ³⁷ but he whom God raised up did not see corruption. ³⁸ Let it be known to you therefore, brothers, that through this man forgiveness of sins is proclaimed to you..."

9.

David's House

2 Samuel 7:1-16; Acts 13:22-23, 32-38 ESV

Two men are sitting around a fire in a majestic wood-paneled room. They are alone, relaxing in comfortable solitude after a long, hard day. One is clearly the "Alpha male." He is tired but contented, and guides the conversation in a quiet, reflective mood. Even here, he exudes that special kind of energy, confidence and charisma that natural leaders all seem to demonstrate when they have reached the pinnacle of success.

The second man listens, patient and attentive, as the first man talks. The second man will speak, but not until he has heard all the other has to say.

The first man is David—*King* David now. His lone companion is a new member of his royal staff—the man responsible for telling David what God wants David—or will allow David—to do. The second man's name is Nathan.

David and Nathan are sitting in the king's new palace. It is a long way, in time and place and experience, from the dark mountain caves where David the fugitive hid from King Saul's search-and-destroy parties, and longer still from the open fields around Bethlehem where young David slept under the stars to protect his father's sheep.

David's House

Now David is a man, living in royal luxury and ruling a still-expanding kingdom. David is a fearsome warrior, a savvy politician, and a man who understands that—for all the trappings of power—he is still subject to the God Who chose him for this remarkable destiny. And all of these aspects of David come into play in this conversation he has initiated with his companion.

"Look here," he says, sweeping his arm around the room, "I'm living in this palace, and the ark of God sits next door in a tent." The implication left unspoken is, "That's not the way it ought to be. Surely God is not happy with this arrangement. I don't want to move out of this palace back into a tent, but I can build a temple for God even better than this house of mine."

And to the unspoken question, Nathan responds, "God is with you. Go and do whatever you want."

And that's how you know Nathan is new at this speaking-for-God business. He didn't bother to check with God to see what God wanted him to say. Oh, he's right about God being with David. That part's a "no-brainer." But God being with you doesn't necessarily mean you can go and do whatever you feel like doing.

֎

Fortunately, Nathan is trainable. When God finally speaks, Nathan listens and passes on the real message of God to the king: "God is with you—and He says 'no.'"

"*No?!*"

"No."

Some things you want—even good and godly things—are not going to happen. David did not build the temple he wanted to build—but God's grace was greater than David's disappointment.

Nathan told David: "God says, 'You will not build Me a house, but I will build you a house.'"

And in that simple promise, the world is changed forever. David won't be able to list the construction of a dazzling temple on his royal resume, but his son will be king after him—by God's

From 2nd Samuel 7

grace—and that son will build that temple—that house for God—or at least for God's *glory*—to dwell in. And as long as there is a kingdom of Judah, a descendant of David will reign as king.

And one day, long after the last of David's line to sit on a throne in Jerusalem is dead and gone, another of David's descendants will come Who will rule, not just over Jerusalem, or Judah, but over all the world—forever. And because that promise, to David, from God, through Nathan, was fulfilled in Jesus Christ, son of David and Son of God, you and I are here today, reflecting on what God has done for us, even as David could reflect on what God had done for him.

Like David, we want to build a house for God.[78] God has not told us *not* to, but as with David, God would have us get a few things straight about this business of building houses.

First of all, God doesn't need the house we want to build for Him, and God will not be kept by us in the house of God we build any more than He would be kept by David or his descendants. All of Creation cannot hold this Creator God, but the house we build will be a place where the God Who has taken us from nothing and made us something will come and dwell with us because He chooses in love to do so.

God does not need this house of God—we do. We will build a house where we will meet and worship our God and we will do it soon and God will cause His glory to dwell with us there, just as He did with the house the son of David and the people of God built for God in Jerusalem.

☙❦

But far more important is what God has promised to build in and for us. God has promised to build you and me into a church—a house of loving, trusting, joyful souls where God causes His Holy

---

[78] During the first three years of this church's existence, we rented various spaces while we were raising money, buying land, developing blueprints and planning to build a dedicated facility.

Spirit to dwell. Whatever we hope to accomplish by building a church will pale in comparison to what God is building in us.

What did God tell David?

"I will appoint a place for My people...and will plant them, that they may dwell in their own place and be disturbed no more. And I will give you rest...."

David wanted to build a house to honor God. But building a beautiful temple would do a lot for David's political career as well. It would turn a lot of heads and make a lot of people sit up and take notice—of David. And to be honest, our building would also bring some practical benefits to Trinity as well: We will likely grow larger and more rapidly when we are in our new church building than we have in this temporary place.

But when we build God's house, we are to build it for His Name—His glory—not ours.

And whatever we use to construct and decorate God's house, the most valuable building materials of God's church will be our faith in Him, and our love for Him and for one another, and our commitment to serve His kingdom together all our days.

What God is building in us will last forever. Whatever we build for God we will share for a time and then pass it on to others. God told David as part of His promise: *"When your days are fulfilled, and you lie down with your ancestors, I will raise up your offspring after you...."*

The fellowship God has built us into will live on in this world beyond each of us. And the spiritual house God is continuing to build in us and in those who will become a part of us as Trinity will dwell with Him in the house we will build for that purpose.

❦

I never met David. I don't know Solomon or any of the other kings of Judah who came and went thousands of years before me. But there is one Son of David Who is my best and closest Friend—the King of the eternal kingdom of which I will always be a part. He is Lord of the house we form by our assembly together—Lord of any building we will erect to glorify His Name. He is Lord of His Father's house in heaven where He says He has prepared a room for you and me.

In my Heavenly Father's house, whether built here by human hands or in heaven by the holy Hands of God Himself, there will always be family fellowship and spiritual food to nourish our souls—bread and wine and brotherly love. And so, as we contemplate the house that we will build for God, let us remember that God has been, and is even now, building His house with us.

2 Samuel 7:1-16 ESV

¹ Now when the king lived in his house and the LORD *had given him rest from all his surrounding enemies, ² the king said to Nathan the prophet, "See now, I dwell in a house of cedar, but the ark of God dwells in a tent." ³ And Nathan said to the king, "Go, do all that is in your heart, for the* LORD *is with you."*

⁴ But that same night the word of the LORD *came to Nathan, ⁵ "Go and tell my servant David, 'Thus says the* LORD*: "Would you build me a house to dwell in? ⁶ I have not lived in a house since the day I brought up the people of Israel from Egypt to this day, but I have been moving about in a tent for my dwelling. ⁷ In all places where I have moved with all the people of Israel, did I speak a word with any of the judges of Israel, whom I commanded to shepherd my people Israel, saying, 'Why have you not built me a house of cedar?'"*

⁸ "Now, therefore, thus you shall say to my servant David, 'Thus says the LORD *of hosts, "I took you from the pasture, from following the sheep, that you should be prince over my people Israel. ⁹ And I have been with you wherever you went and have cut off all your enemies from before you. And I will make for you a great name, like the name of the great ones of the earth. ¹⁰ And I will appoint a place for my people Israel and will plant them, so that they may dwell in their own place and be disturbed no more. And violent men shall afflict them no more, as formerly, ¹¹ from the time that I appointed judges over my people Israel. And I will give you rest from all your enemies. Moreover, the* LORD *declares to you that the* LORD *will make you a house. ¹² When your days are fulfilled and you lie down with your fathers, I will raise up your offspring after you, who shall come from your body, and I will establish his kingdom. ¹³ He shall build a house for my name, and I will establish the throne of his kingdom forever. ¹⁴ I will be to him a father, and he shall be to me a son. When he commits iniquity, I will discipline him with the rod of men, with the stripes of the sons of men, ¹⁵ but my steadfast love will not depart from him, as I took it from Saul, whom I put away from before you. ¹⁶ And your house and your kingdom shall be made sure forever before me. Your throne shall be established forever."'"*

৵৽ঌ

Matthew 7:24-27 ESV

[Jesus said:]

²⁴ "Everyone then who hears these words of mine and does them will be like a wise man who built his house on the rock. ²⁵ And the rain fell, and the floods came, and the winds blew and beat on that house, but it did not fall, because it had been founded on the rock. ²⁶ And everyone who hears these words of mine and does not do them will be like a foolish man who built his house on the sand. ²⁷ And the rain fell, and the floods came, and the winds blew and beat against that house, and it fell, and great was the fall of it."

10.

The Forever House

2 Samuel 7:1-16; Matthew 7:24-27 ESV

King David compiled quite a resume during his rise to royalty and 40 years on the throne. As a shepherd boy, he fought wild animals attacking his flock, and slew a giant with a sling shot, a stone—and the giant's own sword. He could play the harp and sing like an angel, and lead men into battle like a man possessed—a man possessed by the Spirit of God.

As soon as they crowned him king of all Israel, David went and captured Jerusalem and converted it into his capital. Then, he conveyed the ark of the covenant—the symbol of God's presence—to his royal reserve in the city to keep it close by. Over the years, David defeated all the enemies of Israel and expanded her borders in every direction.

But David had one glaring gap in his royal resume: He never built a temple for his God.

He wanted to, of course. David figured out—as King Saul had before him—that *staying* on top is often harder than *getting* on top in the first place. And for that reason, it was a very common thing for a king to construct a temple to show all the people that their king is a godly man and that their god is on his side and that he—

The Forever House

the ruler their god has chosen—will lead them in worship as well as war—and all the other things people look to their leaders to do.

David wanted very much to build a temple. In his case, there was piety as well as politics involved. David had a deep and abiding sense of divine destiny. And the Bible says—time after time as it tells David's story—that *"the Lord was with him."*[79] So David thought, "Why not build God a big house next door to me? It will be like mine—or better."

But it never happened—not on David's watch.

And why was that?

After David's death, his son and successor, Solomon, said it was because his father David had been too busy fighting all his enemies.[80] David's official explanation to Israel was that God wouldn't let him build it because David was a warrior and had shed blood.[81]

But when God speaks to David through the prophet Nathan, God says, "You are not to build Me a temple—a house for Me to live in—because I neither need one nor want one. I never needed a fixed and stationary place, because *I* am not stationary or fixed. I am a God Who goes where I will, and those who want to be with Me will have to follow Me."

"Take up your ark…," God tells the people of Israel and their kings—as Jesus will tell His disciples, *"Take up your cross—and follow me."*[82]

"And besides," God might also have said, "no human house could hold Me. The whole universe isn't big enough for that!"

It's not God Who needs a house, it's David. Just like it's not God who needs this "house"—this church building in which we

---

[79] 1 Samuel 18:12, 14, 28; 2 Samuel 5:10.
[80] 1 Kings 5:2-3.
[81] 1 Chronicles 28:2-3.
[82] Matthew 16:24, NLT.

sit today—it's us. We are the ones who need to have a place where we can come to praise God and pray to Him and hear His Word and have our burdens lifted in His Name.

David needed a house—and so do we. David wasn't sure he could "hold on" as king. After all, his predecessors hadn't. And a "Temple of David" would surely have helped him "strengthen his base"—and his precarious hold on power.

And we wonder sometimes how we can hold on as the world works to wipe us—or our health—or our happiness—away. Surely, having this holy "place" will help make things a little less precarious for us.

But listen to what God says to David about this business of "holy house building." It's kind of like President Kennedy's famous inaugural address turned upside down: "Ask not what you can do for your God. Ask what your God is doing for you."[83] It's like God saying, "You won't build Me a house; I will build you one—a house far greater than you could ever imagine."

God promised to build David a house—meaning not a temple, but a dynasty. The David who wasn't sure he was going to be able to keep on being king was promised that he would rule till he died an old man, and then his son would rule after him and then every king who would ever sit on the royal throne in Jerusalem would be his descendant. And long after there was no longer any kingdom, or throne—long after the last of the temples in Jerusalem was wiped from the face of the earth—a descendent of David would rise to rule the world, and rule it forever.

God told David He would build David a "forever house." And that's exactly what God has done.

---

[83] The line in Kennedy's speech went: "Ask not what your country can do for you—ask what you can do for your country." The sentiment—and much of the wording—were drawn from an 1884 Memorial Day address by Supreme Court Justice (and fellow Massachusetts native) Oliver Wendell Holmes, who said, "…to recall what our country has done for each of us, and to ask ourselves what we can do for our country in return."

After Solomon died, the kingdom David established split in two, but the seat of government for Judah in Jerusalem was always occupied by a descendent of David. After a few centuries, the kingdom David established was destroyed, and foreigners ruled where David and his descendants had. And then, centuries after that, a new and distant descendant of David was born in Bethlehem and became the fulfilment of the final part of that great promise of God: a Son to rule the world—Whose eternal life would extend the reign of David's royal house for all eternity.

Because of God's promise to David to build him a house, God's people began looking at every new royal son to see if he would be the one who would reign forever. And when there were no more kings, they still looked—and even more eagerly—for that special anointed one—the Messiah who would fulfil the promise to David, finally, faithfully and forever.

And one day, some of those seekers found their Messiah in this Man named Jesus, Who was Son of David, as promised—and Son of God, which was far more than the original promise had led anyone to expect.

And what kind of king was—*is*—this last son of David Who has been raised up to rule the world forever—to make the House of David a "forever house"?

He is the King of kings Who washes the feet of those who follow Him[84] so that all may know what God's "forever love" is like. He is the Lord of lords Who lends His back to the lash[85] so that *"by his wounds we* [may be] *healed."*[86] He is the perfect Prince[87] Who pays for our sins[88] by dying our death[89] so that we may live His everlasting life.[90]

---

[84] John 13:5-14.
[85] John 19:1.
[86] Isaiah 53:5, NIV; 1 Peter 2:24.
[87] Hebrews 7:11.
[88] 1 John 2:2
[89] 2 Corinthians 5:21.
[90] John 3:16.

Man-made temples come and go. We raise them up and time tears them, or wears them, down—all of them—sooner or later.

David and Solomon and the rest had their day and they walk no more among us. But the son of David Who is also Son of God said, *"Destroy this temple and in three days I will raise it up."*[91] He is the One of Whom heaven's angels sing, *"The kingdom of the world has become the kingdom of our Lord and of His Christ, and he shall reign forever and ever!"*[92]

And isn't it interesting that David, who was not allowed to build God a house, should finish the psalm that begins, *"The Lord is my shepherd,"* with the words, *"and I will dwell in the house of the Lord forever."*[93]

Will you dwell in the "forever house" God built for David—and for you?

---

[91] John 2:19, RSV.
[92] Revelation 11:15, RSV.
[93] Psalm 23:1, 6, KJV.

2 Samuel 15:13-30 ESV

¹³ And a messenger came to David, saying, "The hearts of the men of Israel have gone after Absalom." ¹⁴ Then David said to all his servants who were with him at Jerusalem, "Arise, and let us flee, or else there will be no escape for us from Absalom. Go quickly, lest he overtake us quickly and bring down ruin on us and strike the city with the edge of the sword." ¹⁵ And the king's servants said to the king, "Behold, your servants are ready to do whatever my lord the king decides." ¹⁶ So the king went out, and all his household after him. And the king left ten concubines to keep the house. ¹⁷ And the king went out, and all the people after him. And they halted at the last house.

¹⁸ And all his servants passed by him, and all the Cherethites, and all the Pelethites, and all the six hundred Gittites who had followed him from Gath, passed on before the king. ¹⁹ Then the king said to Ittai the Gittite, "Why do you also go with us? Go back and stay with the king, for you are a foreigner and also an exile from your home. ²⁰ You came only yesterday, and shall I today make you wander about with us, since I go I know not where? Go back and take your brothers with you, and may the LORD show steadfast love and faithfulness to you." ²¹ But Ittai answered the king, "As the LORD lives, and as my lord the king lives, wherever my lord the king shall be, whether for death or for life, there also will your servant be." ²² And David said to Ittai, "Go then, pass on." So Ittai the Gittite passed on with all his men and all the little ones who were with him. ²³ And all the land wept aloud as all the people passed by, and the king crossed the brook Kidron, and all the people passed on toward the wilderness.

²⁴ And Abiathar came up, and behold, Zadok came also with all the Levites, bearing the ark of the covenant of God. And they set down the ark of God until the people had all passed out of the city. ²⁵ Then the king said to Zadok, "Carry the ark of God back into the city. If I find favor in the eyes of the LORD, he will bring me back and let me see both it and his dwelling place. ²⁶ But if he says, 'I have no pleasure in you,' behold, here I am, let him do to me what seems good to him."

From 2nd Samuel 15

²⁷ The king also said to Zadok the priest, "Are you not a seer? Go back to the city in peace, with your two sons, Ahimaaz your son, and Jonathan the son of Abiathar. ²⁸ See, I will wait at the fords of the wilderness until word comes from you to inform me." ²⁹ So Zadok and Abiathar carried the ark of God back to Jerusalem, and they remained there.

³⁰ But David went up the ascent of the Mount of Olives, weeping as he went, barefoot and with his head covered. And all the people who were with him covered their heads, and they went up, weeping as they went.

Hope in the Darkness

Mark 14:32-36 ESV

³² And they went to a place called Gethsemane. And he said to his disciples, "Sit here while I pray." ³³ And he took with him Peter and James and John, and began to be greatly distressed and troubled. ³⁴ And he said to them, "My soul is very sorrowful, even to death. Remain here and watch." ³⁵ And going a little farther, he fell on the ground and prayed that, if it were possible, the hour might pass from him. ³⁶ And he said, "Abba, Father, all things are possible for you. Remove this cup from me. Yet not what I will, but what you will."

11.

Hope in the Darkness

2 Samuel 15:13-30; Mark 14:32-36 ESV

The geography of old Jerusalem hasn't changed much in two thousand years—or, for that matter, in three. Just as tourists today flock to the Holy Land to walk in the footsteps of Jesus, so Jesus would have been very conscious of the fact that He was walking where His ancestor David had walked, especially when He was in and around Jerusalem.

The architecture was different, of course: There was no temple there in David's day. And much of what David and Solomon had built was gone by the time Jesus got there, replaced by the more recent works of Herod and the Romans. But "the lay of the land" was much the same, with the Kidron Valley dropping off to the east of the Temple Mount, and beyond it, the Garden of Gethsemane nestled at the base of the Mount of Olives.

And both Jesus and David before Him made their way through that valley in their darkest hours, with nothing short of death itself breathing down their necks. And each in his own way would offer the same prayer in that sacred place: "Deliver me from the danger that's closing in on me, if You will, Lord. But regardless, Your will be done."

☙◦❧

We'll come back to Jesus in a moment (as everyone should). But, for now, let's join David as disaster destroys the illusion of his pleasant and well-protected world. Everything is fine, as far as he knows. And then a messenger arrives with very bad news. With one sentence, David's wonderful world is no more.

It can happen that fast.

You've been there. Someone you love says, "I'm leaving." The doctor gives you "the last news in the world you want to hear." Your child goes off the deep end despite all your efforts.

Disaster!

And it's yours, and you've got to live with it.

So what do you do?

You can't turn back the clock or rewind the film. The genie is out of the bottle.

What *can* you do?

❧

David does a number of things when he learns that his son, Absalom, has betrayed him and that the people David had delivered from their oppressors have joined his son in rebellion. These were horrible things to experience. It's the kind of thing that makes you want to roll over and die.

Absalom has *"the men of Israel"* behind him. David has the palace guard and the household staff and a few well-wishers who happen to be in town or hanging out nearby. This time, Chicken Little is right: "The sky *is* falling." And it must feel to King David, "like the moon, the stars and all the planets just fell on [him]"—to borrow Harry Truman's words.[94]

But when David hears the news, he assesses the problem and does what he can do. Hard and heartbreaking as it is, David acts immediately to minimize the impact of what has happened.

---

[94] Harry Truman's first comment to reporters about his reaction to learning of the death of Franklin D. Roosevelt—and his own elevation to the office of President, Washington, DC, April 13, 1945.

From 2nd Samuel 15

He is terribly vulnerable, but David is not alone. In a crisis, some people will step up to help—and some will step out of the line of fire. Bless those who bless you, and let them do for you what they can. And ignore those who drop away. And don't worry about who falls in what category.

David organizes himself, and those who stick with him, for survival, though he cannot guarantee that survival—much less success—will be the result of what they do. He isn't giving up or giving in to despair as he leads those loyal to him out of the city. Like the Marine Corps general at Korea's Chosin Reservoir, surrounded by an overwhelming enemy force, King David is "attacking in a different direction."[95] David is adapting to a new—if undesirable—reality and putting himself in the best position to deal with the mess that has dropped in his lap.

And notice that when he talks about the danger and what must be done about it, all the pronouns are plural:

*"Let **us** flee…or there will be no escape for **us**.…*
*Hurry, or he'll catch **us** and do bad things to **us**."*

Though Absalom is after David and his throne—making the crisis seem very personal—David understands that many people are there to help him, and his darkness is their darkness, too.

David and his people march away from the "old normal" so they can respond better to the "new terrible." With Absalom and his forces on the way, David and his friends walk through the valley of the shadow of death—as we do, when difficulty strikes, and darkness descends upon us.

❧

And here's another thing: Though they do what they have to do without delay, they do not pretend that they like it.

---

[95] Brigadier General Oliver Stone, Commander of the 1st Marine Division, November 1950, though the comment is often attributed to Colonel "Chesty" Puller, who was Commander of the 1st Regiment of the 1st Division at the time.

Hope in the Darkness

When disaster strikes, you grieve, even while you're doing what you can about it—if there's anything you can do.

Everybody is crying. David is crying. They are grown men—strong men—crying out loud—in public! They don't care; their world is coming apart. David and everybody else go out of the city with their feet bare and their heads covered—like mourners going to a funeral. You don't have to act like a catastrophe is "okay" when it's anything but. A good cry about a bad thing can be a good thing.

❧

But here's what I really want you to see: The priests and the Levites bring the ark of the covenant out of Jerusalem so this sacred symbol of God can lead the beleaguered king's impromptu parade. As far as they are concerned, David brought the ark into the city "way back when"; and he has the right to carry it out now. If David has the ark with him—they reason—then, surely, he must have God on his side—or, at least, that's what they want the people who see it and hear about it to think.

But David does an interesting thing: He orders them to take the ark back into the city where they got it.

And David *says* an interesting thing: "If I find favor in the Lord's eyes, He will bring me back and let me see it again."

David's kingdom is coming apart—which would suggest to the casual observer that David has lost any chance of "favor in God's eyes."

The medieval Italian poet Dante wrote a book about the afterlife as he imagined it,[96] and above the entrance to hell was a sign that read, "Abandon all hope, ye who enter here."

You would think a similar sign could have been posted for David as he passed through the gates of his capital city: "Abandon all hope, kings who flee *from* here."

---

[96] Dante Alighieri, *The Divine Comedy*, Part I: "Inferno," 1320.

From 2nd Samuel 15

But David will not take this advice. In his darkest hour—in his most desperate crisis—David lets go of the *symbol* of God in his possession and reaches out for the *reality* of God that neither he nor anyone else can ever possess.

"*If* I find favor with God... I don't know if I will, but I will take my chances with God. I will do everything I can, but I know that, ultimately, it all depends on God, so *I* am depending on God—trusting God in the depths of the darkness."

And *that*, my friends, is what the Bible means by "hope."

ରେ

Why would David put his hope in God?

Yes, David had found favor with God a lot in his life. But over time, David had also done a lot of things that had to have gone in God's "*un*-favorable column."

Is this just David "playing the odds?"

No, this is David, who knows enough about God to believe that hope in this God is a winning strategy in a crisis you can't control yourself: "When I can't make my way work—and things aren't going the way I want them to—I'm willing to go with God."

It's like the song says,

"Through many dangers, toils and snares,
I have already come.
'Tis grace hath brought me safe thus far,
and grace will lead me home."[97]

King David didn't write that song, but he could have.

ରେ

Hope is what allows us to say with the Apostle Paul: *"[W]e are afflicted in every way, but not crushed; perplexed, but not despairing; persecuted, but not forsaken; struck down, but not destroyed...."*[98]

---

[97] John Newton, "Amazing Grace," 1779.
[98] 2 Corinthians 4:8-9, ESV.

Paul also said, *"...we rejoice in hope of the glory of God. Not only that, but we rejoice in our sufferings, knowing that suffering produces endurance, and endurance produces character, and character produces hope, and hope does not put us to shame, because God's love has been poured into our hearts through the Holy Spirit who has been given to us."*[99]

We go into our darkness with hope, and we learn to love the hope and how it helps us in our dark times. And we even come to appreciate that, because of our hope, we can find God and His favor *in* our darkness, sorrow and suffering in a way that we *never* could in "the good times" we prefer.

Did David find the favor with God he hoped for?

Yes, he did. He returned to Jerusalem and his throne—and to the ark.

Did he deserve to find God's favor?

Honestly, no. But that is what hope knows: You can find favor with God without deserving it—because of Who our God is. David should have died, but he didn't. God brought him out of the darkness and back to life...

❦

...which brings us back to David's divine Descendent, Jesus.

Jesus retraces those royal footsteps on the night that He is betrayed. Jesus goes out of the city as far as the Garden of Gethsemane, and there the God in Whom He has put *His* hope orders "Halt!" There in the darkness, a beloved disciple will kiss Him into the hands of His enemies and, ultimately, onto a cross.

Unlike David, Jesus will return to the city the same night He leaves it, and overcome a far worse rebellion than David faced by giving Himself as a sacrifice to those who have sought to kill Him, dying in a darkness that covers not just Him, but the whole

---

[99] Romans 5:2b-5, ESV.

world,[100] finding God's favor in forgiving those who could never find God's favor apart from Him.[101]

David lets go of His hold on Jerusalem, and in the darkness of his despair, puts his hope in God. Jesus lets go of His hold on life, hoping that, in the darkness of death, He will find favor with God.

And now we—who endure the darkness of the hurts and hardships of this life—and death that comes in the end—have the opportunity to put our hope in God, and in doing so, to find His favor, as a restored David and our Risen Lord did.

"Hope does not disappoint"[102]—if you put your hope in God.

---

[100] Matthew 27:45.
[101] Luke 23:34.
[102] Romans 5:5, RSV.

2 Samuel 18:24-33 ESV

^{24} Now David was sitting between the two gates, and the watchman went up to the roof of the gate by the wall, and when he lifted up his eyes and looked, he saw a man running alone. ^{25} The watchman called out and told the king. And the king said, "If he is alone, there is news in his mouth." And he drew nearer and nearer. ^{26} The watchman saw another man running. And the watchman called to the gate and said, "See, another man running alone!" The king said, "He also brings news." ^{27} The watchman said, "I think the running of the first is like the running of Ahimaaz the son of Zadok." And the king said, "He is a good man and comes with good news."

^{28} Then Ahimaaz cried out to the king, "All is well." And he bowed before the king with his face to the earth and said, "Blessed be the LORD your God, who has delivered up the men who raised their hand against my lord the king." ^{29} And the king said, "Is it well with the young man Absalom?" Ahimaaz answered, "When Joab sent the king's servant, your servant, I saw a great commotion, but I do not know what it was." ^{30} And the king said, "Turn aside and stand here." So he turned aside and stood still.

^{31} And behold, the Cushite came, and the Cushite said, "Good news for my lord the king! For the LORD has delivered you this day from the hand of all who rose up against you." ^{32} The king said to the Cushite, "Is it well with the young man Absalom?" And the Cushite answered, "May the enemies of my lord the king and all who rise up against you for evil be like that young man." ^{33} And the king was deeply moved and went up to the chamber over the gate and wept. And as he went, he said, "O my son Absalom, my son, my son Absalom! Would I had died instead of you, O Absalom, my son, my son!"

Luke 15:11-24 ESV

[11] And [Jesus] said, "There was a man who had two sons. [12] And the younger of them said to his father, 'Father, give me the share of property that is coming to me.' And he divided his property between them. [13] Not many days later, the younger son gathered all he had and took a journey into a far country, and there he squandered his property in reckless living. [14] And when he had spent everything, a severe famine arose in that country, and he began to be in need. [15] So he went and hired himself out to one of the citizens of that country, who sent him into his fields to feed pigs. [16] And he was longing to be fed with the pods that the pigs ate, and no one gave him anything.

[17] "But when he came to himself, he said, 'How many of my father's hired servants have more than enough bread, but I perish here with hunger! [18] I will arise and go to my father, and I will say to him, "Father, I have sinned against heaven and before you. [19] I am no longer worthy to be called your son. Treat me as one of your hired servants."'

[20] "And he arose and came to his father. But while he was still a long way off, his father saw him and felt compassion, and ran and embraced him and kissed him. [21] And the son said to him, 'Father, I have sinned against heaven and before you. I am no longer worthy to be called your son.' [22] But the father said to his servants, 'Bring quickly the best robe, and put it on him, and put a ring on his hand, and shoes on his feet. [23] And bring the fattened calf and kill it, and let us eat and celebrate. [24] For this my son was dead, and is alive again; he was lost, and is found.' And they began to celebrate."

12.

Love is Not Enough

2 Samuel 18:24-33, Luke 15:11-24 ESV

Here at Trinity, though we are interdenominational, and expect to disagree, respectfully, about many points of doctrine and practice, we unite in our conviction that the Bible is our supreme written authority for what to believe—and how to behave. But when it comes to behavior, the Bible is just as likely to show us how *not* to behave.

King David, for instance, for all his wonderful accomplishments, could conduct a clinic in how *not* to be a father. His inconsolable cries of despair at the news of Absalom's death are but the closing curtain on the long and tragic drama of this troubled relationship between famous father and son.

What did David do wrong with Absalom?

The list is long and starts even before Absalom was born. A full 15 chapters before we are told of his death, the Bible introduces Absalom[103] by saying his mother was a foreign princess (who, we may presume, did not believe in or submit to David's God). And yet, God had commanded His people, "Do not get involved with foreign women who are not involved with Me."[104]

---

[103] 2 Samuel 3:2-3.
[104] Deuteronomy 7:1-4.

But that was just the beginning.

As Absalom was growing up, David ignored his sacred responsibility to be the moral leader of his family and his people. He allowed himself to be seduced by—or, perhaps, to himself seduce—or worse—a woman he knew to be the wife of one of his most loyal soldiers—and the daughter of another.[105] In that moment, David did not care about God's will, or his loyalty to his warrior band of brothers, or how his immorality would undermine his ability to rule the kingdom. He just decided he would "have" her—and that's what he did.

He tried to cover up what he'd done. When he failed at that, David used his royal power—that God had given him—to cause the cold-blooded killing of his devoted servant, Uriah, and others.[106]

Later, when another son, Amnon, followed his father's immoral example, David ignored his duty to protect his own daughter (and Absalom's sister) from sexual assault—or at least to punish Amnon for forcing himself upon her.[107] David's acceptance of injustice drove Absalom to take justice into his own hands and kill his brother, rocking the kingdom again in the process.[108]

David made a habit of ignoring Absalom—before he killed Amnon and ran away from home, during his years in exile in his mother's country,[109] and after David let him return to Israel.[110]

David ignored his royal responsibility to render justice in his country as he had ignored it in his family, and after his return from exile, Absalom usurped this role because his father had shirked it.[111]

---

[105] 2 Samuel 11:2-3; 23:8a, 24a, 34b, 39.
[106] 2 Samuel 11:6-17.
[107] 2 Samuel 13:1-22.
[108] 2 Samuel 13:23-29.
[109] 2 Samuel 13:37-38.
[110] 2 Samuel 14:21-24.
[111] 2 Samuel 15:2-6.

David ignored the obvious signs that his son was growing vain, arrogant, deceptive and increasingly rebellious against him. Yet David did not challenge Absalom or correct him.

Only when Absalom has become a full-fledged enemy is there any indication that David cares for the one he referred to most often as (merely) *"the young man."*[112] And only when he discovers that Absalom is dead does David give way to gut-wrenching grief, bewailing the loss of his beloved son.

Did David love his son, Absalom?

It appears so here, in the end, when tragedy reigns instead of Absalom or David. But love is not enough. And certainly here, it is too late. His father's love could not save Absalom from the hatred of the other enemies he had made when he chose to rise up in rebellion against his father. David's love for Absalom could not bring his son back from the dead.

❧

So what can fathers learn from David's failures?

God told the children of Israel repeatedly, "Leave those foreign women with foreign religions alone. They will lead you astray."[113] Later, early Christians were counseled, *"Do not be unequally yoked with unbelievers."*[114]

The time for a father to start loving his children is long before they are born, by considering carefully what kind of woman God wants their mother to be. Would a truly loving father-to-be risk the future of his children by getting involved with a woman who is foreign to his faith—who will not agree with him or work with him to instill the knowledge and love of the Lord in their children from the day they are born?

The answer is "no," and that is Lesson One.

---

[112] 2 Samuel 14:21; 18:5, 32.
[113] Deuteronomy 7:1-4.
[114] 2 Corinthians 6:14, ESV.

David (unfortunately) led by example, as all fathers will, whether they mean to or not. And because we all lead by example, every father is responsible to form himself into an example worth following long before there are any children to follow him. David did not do this.

Today, we live in a culture where boys are not being raised to be husbands of wives and fathers of children—"producers" of children, yes—seekers of physical pleasure with women, yes—but also addicts to their own desires, gratifiers of their own egos and avoiders (or "postponers") of every man's true, basic responsibility to establish and provide a stable, nurturing, godly home for a family—if God so grants it—so that children will have the greatest opportunity to grow up in a way that will not ruin their lives and break their parents' hearts in the end.

What we model to our children, most of the time, are the habits—good and bad—that we have developed over the course of a lifetime—the ways that are the result of countless daily decisions and even more automatic actions and impulses that we never consider at all. And thus, a boy becomes a man who will show his children "something" about how to live their lives. But does he do anything along the way to make that "something" what it ought to be?

Let every man and boy ask himself each day, "Who will I become if I do this thing I want so much to do right now? And who will my children become if they grow up doing what I do—following my example—or rejecting the example I have become because they cannot respect it?"

Let us say that David loved Absalom. But the truth is that until the day that Absalom died, David loved himself more. David put his own desires above Absalom's needs—needs for attention and affirmation, for structure and even discipline, for love and

From 2nd Samuel 18

respect—and for a father figure that a son could love and respect in return.

The story of David and Absalom is long and contorted. It weaves its way through a maze of missteps that ends in the agony of a father who finds—too late—that he would have died for the son who is now dead—the son he cannot bring back. It is a cautionary tale for every father who floats through life without devoting himself to being, or becoming, the kind of father his children need him to be.

But David's is not the only "father story" in the Bible. Jesus told about a father who, like David, had a son who rebelled against him—a son who, like Absalom, did something very bad and ran way to a foreign land for his safety. Like Absalom, this parable son—this prodigal son—rebelled against his father and it got him killed—almost.

Though both of these sons went into exile, Absalom was able to live in the luxury of a foreign palace, while the unnamed son found himself, finally, starving in a pig sty. The other difference was that this latter son came to his senses before it was too late: He went back to his father.

And here's where the fathers were different: When Absalom was allowed to come back from exile, his father David ignored him. When the other son came back, Jesus says the father ran to him and hugged him and kissed him and showered him with valuable signs of love—and he made sure everyone came to celebrate with him his son's return.

If Absalom had been brought back alive from the battle in which he died, no doubt David would have killed, not just the fatted calf, but the whole herd, and welcomed everyone in the whole country to the feast. But when he actually had the chance to celebrate Absalom's earlier return, David didn't take even one step in his son's direction. He didn't shed even one tear of joy or crack a smile in relief or pleasure that his son had come home. And as they say at the end of some movies, "no animals were harmed" in

Love is Not Enough

the preparation for Absalom's "Welcome Home" feast—because no such feast was ever held.

The father Jesus told about was afraid his son was dead. He knew his son was lost and that, whatever his son's circumstances, he—the father—could not save him.

This is a father who is focused on his children and loves them, even when they are not perfect. He endures their anger, greed, stupidity, disrespect and lack of love for him—in order to be the example of a father's proper love for them. Here is a father giving his children more than love. And even though he could not bring them back from the dead, he can—and will—celebrate with all his heart when one does come back.

Many would say he is a "model" father. But he is an imaginary father—a character in a parable told by Jesus.

ঔ∞ঙ

But this unnamed father of this unnamed son is himself modeled on another Father—a real Father—Whose Name *is* known and was often spoken—in love and respect and confidence—by Jesus Himself, when He prayed to this Father and presented Him to all the Father's lost, rebellious and dying children—who have your name and mine.

He is the Father of a Son Who went from His Father's home to a faraway place—not in arrogant rebellion, but in humble obedience—to die at the hands of those rebellious children who thought they were doing this Father a favor by killing His beloved Son.[115] And though David wanted, in the end, to die in the place of his sinful son, the Heavenly Father sent His sinless Son to die in the place of all His sinful brothers and sisters whose earthly fathers could never die for them or bring them back from the dead.[116]

---

[115] Philippians 2:5-8.
[116] 1 John 4:9-10.

From 2nd Samuel 18

David could not bring Absalom back—to his unbearable sorrow. The prodigal's father could not have brought his son back, either, though, in the end, he did not have to—to his uncontainable joy. But the Heavenly Father did bring His Son, Jesus, back from the dead—and will do the same for all the sons and daughters and mothers and fathers who believe in Him.[117]

When our love, by itself, is not enough, our Heavenly Father's love is all—and always—sufficient, for in it are all His power and peace, His justice and His mercy, and the grace to bring us back from death and rebellion and the faraway places we have gone to get away from Him.

The Father rejoices when prodigals return.

The Father rejoices when sinful children are saved.

Happy Father's Day, O God and Father of us all!

---

[117] 1 Peter 1:20-21, Romans 8:11.

2 Samuel 23:1-2 RSV

King David was, in his lifetime, shepherd, soldier, sovereign—and psalmist. He played a musical instrument, composed songs, and set up the musical component of Israel's worship. David, more than any other person, taught God's people *how* to worship, and provided us the timeless tools of prayer and praise.

¹ Now these are the last words of David:
The oracle of David, the son of Jesse,
the oracle of the man who was raised on high,
the anointed of the God of Jacob,
the sweet psalmist of Israel:
² "The Spirit of the LORD *speaks by me,*
his word is upon my tongue.

Colossians 3:12-17 RSV

Paul tells early believers that singing the songs of their faith is to be a central part of the way they are to express and celebrate their relationship with God and their fellowship with other Christians.

[12] *Put on then, as God's chosen ones, holy and beloved, compassion, kindness, lowliness, meekness, and patience,* [13] *forbearing one another and, if one has a complaint against another, forgiving each other; as the Lord has forgiven you, so you also must forgive.* [14] *And above all these put on love, which binds everything together in perfect harmony.* [15] *And let the peace of Christ rule in your hearts, to which indeed you were called in the one body. And be thankful.* [16] *Let the word of Christ dwell in you richly, teach and admonish one another in all wisdom, and sing psalms and hymns and spiritual songs with thankfulness in your hearts to God.* [17] *And whatever you do, in word or deed, do everything in the name of the Lord Jesus, giving thanks to God the Father through him.*

13.

Sing to God

2 Samuel 23:1-2; Colossians 3:12-17 RSV

How are you feeling today?

As I expected, because you know I am preaching a sermon—and because I have asked the question in a roomful of people—you are not inclined to answer me.

If, on the other hand, we met each other somewhere, you would recognize the question for the friendly greeting it is, and you would answer. You would probably say, "Fine," which is the standard reply. Or perhaps, because I am a pastor, you might let me know about a bit of bursitis or some allergies that are acting up.

But we don't usually talk about our "feelings," even when asked, because we're not really being asked about them, most of the time. It's just another way to say "hello."

ஐ‑ஒ

But today, the question is not just a friendly conventional greeting. Not that I'm expecting a verbal answer from you all, but I do want to talk about your feelings—*how* you're "feeling"—*what* you're "feeling"—and what you do about it.

Each of you is feeling something right now. And I'm not just talking about the temperature in the room or your reaction to what I've had to say so far. You came to church with feelings…got up this morning with feelings…went through the events of this past week with feelings. We live our lives with feelings.

What are you feeling just now?

That's easier to imagine for some than it is for others.

Someone with a new baby is feeling great joy and pride. Someone with a sick loved one is feeling concern, and sorrow and fear perhaps. Someone may be feeling sick about the state of the family finances—or the state of a relationship—or the state of the country. Sitting in your seat, going through the order of worship, listening to the sermon—you are feeling your own personal experience of life and all that entails for you.

You're doing what all of us do: You're "feeling"—and thinking and wondering and worrying and wishing that something in your life was different. Or if you're lucky, you really *are* feeling "fine"— or better than fine—because life can be good as well as bad.

We are "feeling" creatures—whether we express our feelings or not. And our lives give us so much to feel about. Life is a journey marked both by dependable unchanging constants and a never-ending combination of unexpected difficulties and equally unexpected blessings. And all of this, so the Bible says, is experienced in relation to God—Who created us and installed in us all the feelings we feel as we make our way through the lives that are ours.

We live our lives in relation to this God—this remarkable God—whether we know it or admit it or not. And we feel our feelings in relation to Him as well. It's as though God is constantly asking: "How are you feeling?" With God, it's not just friendly chit-chat. God wants you to share your feelings—your experience of the specific events of your life—with Him.

How do I know?

The Bible tells me so.

And I'm not referring now just to a passage or two, but to a whole book of the Bible—the biggest book of the Bible—and more.

ೞ

When King David, an accomplished musician in his own right, set up the musical component of the worship of Israel, he provided his people and the world a divinely-inspired resource of unequaled power for communicating with God about how we feel about the lives we are living, and the things we are experiencing, and how all of that plays into our relationship with God.

There are some 150 psalms in the Book of Psalms and dozens more scattered throughout the rest of the Bible. And for more than 2,000 years, these psalms have done more to calm fears and generate courage and mend broken hearts and sustain faith, to equip people to live—and die—in communion with God, than any other words known to man. They have been the songs and prayers of God's people from the time of David to the time of Jesus and all the way up to this day and this moment.

We often conclude our scripture readings with the affirmation: "The Word of God for the people of God." We could go farther with The Psalms: "These are the words of God for the people of God to use when speaking to God."

ೞ

These are the words God has given you for those times when your grief is so deep or your joy so high that you cannot find the words within yourself to express what you feel, but what you feel is so strong that you must find a way to express it or you will explode—or implode. These are the words for the times when your life is coming apart and you cannot see how it will ever come back together—when everything you value or love is gone, and you know it is gone forever.

The words of The Psalms are powerful words because they are God's words. They give us permission to speak in the presence of the Holy—directly to God. They speak a language that does not require translation—that loses nothing in transmission. The Psalms allow us—encourage us—to be bold—audacious—in speaking to God—to put away the pretense and get to the point—to the truth about what we're feeling and what we want and need from God.

There are certainly psalms that celebrate the wonders and character of God—His grace and mercy and steadfast love. But there are also psalms that challenge God to act like God should act—and quickly—demanding to know why God is taking so long to do what His own divine nature requires Him to do—not because the speaker deserves God's intervention, but because God's reputation demands that He act—to save—to protect—to redeem—to provide for His people—to right wrongs and renew hope.

It would be risky to say to God what the psalmists say—if the presence of these words in the Bible did not assure us that God allows it. But we pray to a God Who has revealed Himself to us in the words He gives us, and His words mark the way where we may safely walk in prayer.

And walk we have—with remarkable results.

༄༅

The psalms in the Bible are both the model and the permit for prayer. They are also the archives of answered prayer.

The psalms in the Bible are there, all these centuries later, because they "work." Those who penned them under the inspiration of God's Holy Spirit—and all those who, in countless generations after, offered them to God, in private and in public—are the guarantors of their power to touch the heart of God and to energize His mighty arm on behalf of His people.

From 2nd Samuel 23

And we, in this day, who have ourselves experienced the power of these psalms to comfort and keep us against the depths of despair and the dark shadows of death extend the testimony of their effectiveness to the present. Time and time again, some poor soul feels that all he can do is cry out to the Lord—in agony, in fear, in hopelessness—and he does cry out, in the words of a lament or prayer for deliverance.

And God hears him.

☙❧

And then prayer becomes praise.

You see, the psalms also provide the right words for the times when the life you thought you had lost—the life you knew was over—comes to life again—against all odds. God gives you words to speak to Him when He alone can do what must be done.

And when you realize He *has* done just that—just exactly what you want and need most, and never imagined possible—even with God (Oh, ye of little faith!)—He gives you words that will enable you to give worthy voice to those new, spectacular miraculous feelings that no words of your own can do justice to.

The Book of Psalms is the prayer book of God's people—and our first song book. God wants us to pray, and teaches us how, so that we can express what we are feeling to Him with a power we do not possess. But to pray properly and powerfully in our pain or sorrow or fear or anger is only part of the process of our relationship with God.

We are to praise Him—to sing songs of praise for His
    goodness
    and mercy
    and steadfast love
    and faithfulness
    and justice
    and grace—

for deliverance from enemies—
for protection from evil—
for freedom instead of bondage—
for abundance instead of want—
for reconciliation that overcame separation—
for salvation when we faced destruction—
for life in place of death.

God has given us the words to express our feelings of gratitude and joy and fulfilled hope—so that we do not forget to feel those things when the reasons for feeling the bad things of this life are taken away by God. God gives us the words and the opportunities to praise Him so that we may realize that God often takes away our sorrow, pain and fears through our singing His praise. He gives us good things to feel in the midst of what would otherwise make us feel bad—*if* we will give ourselves and our feelings over to Him in faith. And then, He gives us the words to describe what God has done and to celebrate it: glory and praise. "Thank you, Lord" and "Halleluiah!" which, of course, is the Hebrew word for "Praise the Lord!"

ಸಂ

There are times when we must cry out to God—our lives and our feelings demand it. And there are times when we must sing God's praise—our hearts are too full with joy to do anything else. Too many people suffer in silence because they do not have the words to pour out their hearts before the Lord. Too many people squelch the joy within them because they will not sing God's praise. Whatever your feeling, God has provided the words to express it to Him. The Psalms are yours for the taking—yours for the praying—yours for praising. It only waits for you to find the words—the psalms—that match your feelings and make them your own—your own prayers—your own songs—your own word *from* God *to* God.

ಸಂ

From the Book of 1st Kings

What Shall God Give You?

1 Kings 2:10-12; 3:3-14 NRSV

2 ¹⁰ Then David slept with his fathers and was buried in the city of David. ¹¹ And the time that David reigned over Israel was forty years. He reigned seven years in Hebron and thirty-three years in Jerusalem. ¹² So Solomon sat on the throne of David his father, and his kingdom was firmly established.

3 ³ Solomon loved the Lord, walking in the statutes of David his father, only he sacrificed and made offerings at the high places. ⁴ And the king went to Gibeon to sacrifice there, for that was the great high place. Solomon used to offer a thousand burnt offerings on that altar. ⁵ At Gibeon the Lord appeared to Solomon in a dream by night, and God said, "Ask what I shall give you." ⁶ And Solomon said, "You have shown great and steadfast love to your servant David my father, because he walked before you in faithfulness, in righteousness, and in uprightness of heart toward you. And you have kept for him this great and steadfast love and have given him a son to sit on his throne this day. ⁷ And now, O Lord my God, you have made your servant king in place of David my father, although I am but a little child. I do not know how to go out or come in. ⁸ And your servant is in the midst of your people whom you have chosen, a great people, too many to be numbered or counted for multitude. ⁹ Give your servant therefore an understanding mind to govern your people, that I may discern between good and evil, for who is able to govern this your great people?"

¹⁰ It pleased the Lord that Solomon had asked this. ¹¹ And God said to him, "Because you have asked this, and have not asked for yourself long life or riches or the life of your enemies, but have asked for yourself understanding to discern what is right, ¹² behold, I now do according to your word. Behold, I give you a wise and discerning mind, so that none like you has been before you and none like you shall arise after you. ¹³ I give you also what you have not asked, both riches and honor, so that no other king shall compare with you, all your days. ¹⁴ And if you will walk in my ways, keeping my statutes and my commandments, as your father David walked, then I will lengthen your days."

☙❧

14.

What Shall God Give You?

1 Kings 2:10-12; 3:3-14 NRSV

The campaign is over.[118] There was a clear winner. The outcome could not have been predicted when all the political maneuvering began. But a coalition of shrewd and determined people worked the system like the consummate professionals they were, and the result was a stunning victory for their man. He is young, charismatic, popular as a rock star, and he's full of big plans for the country.

He won the campaign for office. He's the guy in change. But, as with all successful politicians, he now has to do something harder: He has to govern. His name is Solomon, and from this point, he will go on to be the brightest, wealthiest, most spectacular failure in the Bible.

The passages from 1st Kings we heard today come from the beginning of Solomon's reign and read like press releases from his public affairs office: "The great King David has died and his son, Solomon, who served for a time as his co-regent, is firmly established as the new king and head of government."

---

[118] This sermon was preached after the 2008 election.

What Shall God Give You?

Note that it says Solomon is *"firmly established."* This is important. They've had their first transfer of power within the house of David and there are no serious challenges to the throne, which means no civil war, anarchy or chaos will descend upon the nation. With peace, there is the hope of prosperity. Great things may be anticipated.

The new king is being introduced to his subjects. They learn that their new king loves God and is loved by Him. The new king worships God publicly and puts some significant resources into the effort when he does. The new king has had a personal encounter with God, the details of which are published for widest distribution among his subjects. According to the king, God appeared to him in a dream and commanded him to ask God for a gift for his inauguration. The exact words are: *"Ask what I shall give you."*

Imagine what God could give him. Solomon can have anything God has to give, and there is nothing God does not have to give. If you could have anything you wanted, what would it be?

More to the point: What does a king want? What does a king need? What will Solomon ask for?

He ponders his choice while he offers some appropriately humble comments to God about God's generosity and his own deficiencies. And then he chooses.

Solomon says, *"Give me an understanding mind to govern Your people…"* Make me *"able to discern between good and evil."*

And God is pleased with what Solomon has requested. Knowing what Solomon could have asked for, God in His overwhelmingly generous way promises to give him far more than what he has asked for. God promises to give Solomon the understanding he has requested: perceptive insight—the ability to analyze and reason.

But God also promises wisdom: prudence, moral sensitivity, spiritual awareness, the skills for administering matters of state—a significant upgrade on your basic understanding package. And then

God throws in wealth and honor, two very big-ticket items Solomon had the good sense *not* to ask for.

At this point, I remind you of that technical term I taught you last year: MOLAB.[119] Do you remember MOLAB? It stands for "made out like a bandit." This is a "MOLAB moment" for Solomon. He has "made out like a bandit" in this nighttime encounter with God. God is remarkably generous. Solomon has been remarkably blessed.

☙❧

But here, as everywhere, there is an "if." "*If,*" says God, "*you will walk in My ways, keeping My statutes and commands…*" All will be well—if. All this—and more—will be yours—if.

Just the one "if." But by the 11th Chapter of 1st Kings, the God Who established Solomon as king is now angry with Solomon and is about to tear the kingdom from his hand. God gave Solomon the understanding and wisdom he asked for, but he turned his heart away from God.

When Solomon became king, his kingdom was *"firmly established."* By the time he died, his reputation for material magnificence was firmly established—and his kingdom was destroyed.

God gave him the capacity for wisdom and Solomon used it to enhance his personal glory and impress his international entourage with his cleverness. God gave Solomon wealth, but God's wealth wasn't enough for him, so Solomon took what belonged to his people and used it to maintain an unprecedented lifestyle of extravagance. God gave Solomon the honor of building God's Temple, but he dishonored God and his country and himself by building other temples to all the gods of all the foreign wives he married.

---

[119] I introduced the term in the sermon, "What Did You Get for Christmas?" in the book, *O Come, Let God Adore Us.*

Under Solomon, the children of Israel, God's chosen people, became merely a well-regimented and overtaxed source of free labor, forced to build his great buildings and supply the food for his massive royal household. And the kingdom Solomon built on their backs collapsed with his death. Solomon may have been the most foolish wise man who ever lived.

❧❧

Now, if this were a mere historical curiosity, I would not have brought it up. You've got more to worry about these days than old dead kings—even kings as dazzling as Solomon. But Solomon's failure is not just an irrelevant "factoid" from the foggy past.

God said to Solomon, *"Ask what I shall give you."*

And Jesus says to His disciples, *"If you abide in me, and my words abide in you, ask whatever you wish, and it will be done for you"*[120] and *"very truly I tell you, my Father will give you whatever you ask in my name."*[121]

You and I have been offered the same deal as Solomon.

"YES, SIR. HALLELUIAH! NAME IT AND CLAIM IT! GOD'S GOT THE GOODIES AND YOU NEED TO GET YOURS! JUST STEP UP AND TELL GOD WHAT YOU WANT!"

No, that's called "The Prosperity Gospel," and it is heresy. The Bible says, *"When you ask, you do not receive, because you ask with wrong motives, that you may spend what you get on your pleasures."*[122]

Notice that Jesus said, "If…"

"If you abide in me and my words abide in you…" and *"…if you ask in my name."*

"If…"

But God did say, *"Ask what I shall give you."* And Jesus does say, *"Ask whatever you wish in my name and my Father will give it to you."*[123]

---

[120] John 15:7, NASB.
[121] John 16:23, NIV.
[122] James 4:3, NIV.
[123] John 16:23, ESV.

From 1st Kings 2 and 3

So what shall you ask for? What shall God give you?

When God gave Solomon the chance to choose what God would give him, Solomon chose well—but he did not choose well enough. Solomon chose a good and worthy thing, but when God gave it to him, Solomon took God's good gift and perverted it because of his sinful human inclinations.

It would have been even easier to pervert gifts like wealth or glory or power. Our basic human sinfulness is able and inclined to misuse and abuse just about anything God gives us, whatever our good intentions.

❦

So what shall you ask God for, as you sit here in this holy place? What shall you ask God for, in the quiet of your own home?

What shall God give you when He comes to you in the solitude of sleep or the privacy of your hidden heart and says, "Ask!"?

What can God give you that will not tarnish in your hands or be turned to sinful purpose in your mind?

Ask for the "if…"

Suppose Solomon had asked for the "if." Suppose Solomon had made his highest desire that one thing that everything else depended on. Remember?

God said, *"I give you a wise and understanding mind…. I give you riches and honor and long life…if—if you will walk in My ways, keeping My statutes and My commandments…."*

Suppose Solomon had said, "O Lord my God, You have made Your servant king, but anything You give me, my sinful nature will turn to some selfish end. So give me, instead, the will to walk in Your ways at all times. Give me the courage and character to keep Your statutes and Your commandments at all times, come what may. Give me such a spirit of submission and obedience to Your Word that I will never turn away from You or do what is evil in Your sight."

What Shall God Give You?

If Solomon had said that, he would have sounded a good bit more like another son of David Who, centuries later, said to His disciples, *"I have come down from heaven not to do my will, but to do the will of him who sent me."*[124]

And what did this later son of David ask God to give?

"I will ask the Father, and he will give you another Counselor to be with you forever…the Spirit of truth…."[125]

So let's review:

Jesus says, *"If you…though you are evil, know how to give good gifts to your children, how much more will your Father in heaven give good gifts to those who ask him!"*[126] Jesus says, *"Ask and it will be given to you."*[127]

So what shall God give you?

Imagine what God *could* give you. You can have anything God has to give, and there is nothing God does not have to give. If you could have anything you wanted, what would it be?

But that's the wrong question. That's what got Solomon into trouble. He didn't ask for a *bad* thing. He asked for a *good* thing. But he did not ask for the *best* thing.

What is the best thing you can ask for—the right thing to request?

Maybe the words of a little praise chorus have the answer:

"Lord, make me like You.
Please make me like You.
You are a servant;
Make me one, too.
O Lord, I am willing;
Do what You must do
To make me like You, Lord,
Just make me like You."[128]

---

[124] John 6:38, ESV.
[125] John 14:16-17, RSV.
[126] Matthew 7:11, NIV.
[127] Matthew 7:7, NIV.
[128] Jimmy and Carol Owens, "Make Me Like You," 1978.

It's like Jesus says, *"Seek ye first the kingdom of God, and His righteousness, and all these things shall be added unto you."*[129]

What shall God give you?

If you are wise, you will ask God to give you what He most wants you to have.

Go ahead: Ask Him.

Now to him who is able to do immeasurably more than all we ask or imagine, according to his power that is at work within us, to him be glory in the church and in Christ Jesus throughout all generations, for ever and ever! Amen.[130]

---

[129] Matthew 6:33, KJV.
[130] Ephesians 3:20-21, NIV.

In the House of the Lord

1 Kings 6:1, 7, 11-13, 19-21, 37-38; 8:6-11 ESV

King Solomon, the son of David, was allowed by God to build the Temple in Jerusalem that God would not let David build during his reign.

꙳

6 *¹ In the four hundred and eightieth year after the people of Israel came out of the land of Egypt, in the fourth year of Solomon's reign over Israel, in the month of Ziv, which is the second month, he began to build the house of the* LORD

⁷ When the house was built, it was with stone prepared at the quarry, so that neither hammer nor axe nor any tool of iron was heard in the house while it was being built.

¹¹ Now the word of the LORD *came to Solomon, ¹² "Concerning this house that you are building, if you will walk in my statutes and obey my rules and keep all my commandments and walk in them, then I will establish my word with you, which I spoke to David your father. ¹³ And I will dwell among the children of Israel and will not forsake my people Israel."*

¹⁹ The inner sanctuary he prepared in the innermost part of the house, to set there the ark of the covenant of the LORD. *²⁰ The inner sanctuary was twenty cubits long, twenty cubits wide, and twenty cubits high, and he overlaid it with pure gold. He also overlaid an altar of cedar. ²¹ And Solomon overlaid the inside of the house with pure gold, and he drew chains of gold across, in front of the inner sanctuary, and overlaid it with gold.*

³⁷ In the fourth year the foundation of the house of the LORD *was laid, in the month of Ziv. ³⁸ And in the eleventh year, in the month of Bul, which is the eighth month, the house was finished in all its parts, and according to all its specifications. He was seven years in building it.*

From 1st Kings 6 and 8

8 *⁶ Then the priests brought the ark of the covenant of the* LORD *to its place in the inner sanctuary of the house, in the Most Holy Place, underneath the wings of the cherubim. ⁷ For the cherubim spread out their wings over the place of the ark, so that the cherubim overshadowed the ark and its poles. ⁸ And the poles were so long that the ends of the poles were seen from the Holy Place before the inner sanctuary; but they could not be seen from outside. And they are there to this day. ⁹ There was nothing in the ark except the two tablets of stone that Moses put there at Horeb, where the* LORD *made a covenant with the people of Israel, when they came out of the land of Egypt. ¹⁰ And when the priests came out of the Holy Place, a cloud filled the house of the* LORD, *¹¹ so that the priests could not stand to minister because of the cloud, for the glory of the* LORD *filled the house of the* LORD.

In the House of the Lord

1 Corinthians 3:9-17 ESV

Paul tells early believers that a central part of their relationship with God and their fellowship with other Christians is to be expressed in singing the songs of their faith.

⁹ For we are God's fellow workers. You are God's field, God's building.

¹⁰ According to the grace of God given to me, like a skilled master builder I laid a foundation, and someone else is building upon it. Let each one take care how he builds upon it. ¹¹ For no one can lay a foundation other than that which is laid, which is Jesus Christ. ¹² Now if anyone builds on the foundation with gold, silver, precious stones, wood, hay, straw— ¹³ each one's work will become manifest, for the Day will disclose it, because it will be revealed by fire, and the fire will test what sort of work each one has done. ¹⁴ If the work that anyone has built on the foundation survives, he will receive a reward. ¹⁵ If anyone's work is burned up, he will suffer loss, though he himself will be saved, but only as through fire.

¹⁶ Do you not know that you are God's temple and that God's Spirit dwells in you? ¹⁷ If anyone destroys God's temple, God will destroy him. For God's temple is holy, and you are that temple.

15.

In the House of the Lord

1 Kings 6:1, 7, 11-13, 19-21, 37-38 and 8:6-11; 1 Corinthians 3:9-17 ESV

In the spring of his fourth year as king of Israel—ruler of the 12 tribes and all the territories his father David had subdued—Solomon pushed the ceremonial shovel into the ground on Mount Zion and officially began the construction of a temple for the God of his people.

It took seven years to complete the project, which was the most important thing that had ever happened in the history of Jerusalem. And it would remain the most important thing for almost a thousand years—right up till the day when a descendent of Solomon was nailed to a cross there for saying, among other things, *"Destroy this temple, and I will raise it again in three days."*[131]

The Bible goes to great lengths in describing the details of the temple Solomon built. The dimensions are very specific; the materials are listed, space by space, as are the decorations.

Solomon seems to have spared no expense in building this house for his Lord. He covered walls from floor to ceiling in pure gold. The finest wood from the forests of Lebanon covered

---

[131] John 2:19, NIV.

whatever the gold didn't. And most of the splendor—the public would never see.

Solomon built a brand-new house for the Lord. It was supposed to prove that God was on his side—that God had put a sacred stamp of approval on Solomon's reign—that God would always take care of Solomon and his kingdom. But God wasn't as impressed by the building as everyone else seemed to be. God told Solomon, "I'll come here, and be with you and your people—*if!*"

The temple Solomon built was never going to control God's presence or His actions, but if the king and the people were obedient to the word God had given them centuries before, when all there was to worship in was a temporary tent in the desert, then God would come into this house of the Lord, and cause His Spirit to dwell there, and be their God.

And notice something else: When this brand-new building was finished and was full of everything Solomon's wealth and power could come up with to fill it, it was still empty and useless as far as real temples go—because *God* wasn't in it.

And God wasn't there because the building was missing one crucial piece of equipment: an old box that had been carried around from place to place for centuries, with nothing in it but a couple of carved up stones from the Sinai desert. We know the box as the ark of the covenant and the stones as the Ten Commandments.

The ark was to be "the temple within the Temple"—THE DWELLING PLACE OF GOD within The Dwelling Place of God. If God chose to cause His Spirit to come and rest on the ark as He had in the past, then the whole Temple would become that holy place Solomon and the people desperately wanted it, and built it, to be.

And so, after the house of the Lord was completed, Solomon had the priests bring the ark into the place that was to be the holiest spot in the Temple. No one would see it, except the high priest, and even then, only on rare occasions. But because the ark was in

From 1ˢᵗ Kings 6 and 8

the Temple, God chose to come and be with it—to hover over it. And because He did, the whole place was filled with the cloud of the glory of God. Because God was there, in "the temple within the Temple," the house of the Lord became a holy place.

☙❧

Now come with me to the New Testament.

Another temple has taken the place of the one Solomon built. Solomon's Temple was destroyed because the people and their leaders were disobedient, despite God's warning, beginning with Solomon and his generation. In time, God abandoned the people and the house they had built for Him. Enemies burned it to the ground.

By the time of Jesus, the replacement Temple in Jerusalem was once again a big deal.

But the ark of the covenant was long gone, and the presence of the glory and Spirit of God was a very "iffy" thing. A lot of the locals were pretty obsessive about their beloved Temple in Jesus' day, but it also had become a prime location for the retail currency and livestock trade.

Was God present in that temple?

It was hard to tell—unless this mysterious, charismatic Carpenter from Nazareth happened to be there. And because the Spirit of God was with Him—in Him—when Jesus was in the Temple, the Spirit of God was in the Temple, too. God was again in "the temple within the Temple," for the temple Jesus was talking about being destroyed was His own Body.

And it was destroyed. They crucified Jesus—took the human life and the Holy Spirit out of His Body.

And three days later, God put it back. Later still, when Jesus ascended into heaven, God sent His Spirit—*poured* His Holy Spirit—into other bodies—other "temples."

Paul said to the disciples of Jesus in Corinth, *"you are God's temple...God's Spirit dwells in you...God's temple is holy, and you are that temple."*

Jesus had said, *"...where two or three are gathered in my name, there am I among them."*[132]

And Paul again: *"In him, you, too, are being built together to become a dwelling in which God lives by his Spirit."*[133]

Because of the crucifixion and resurrection of Jesus and the pouring out of the Holy Spirit upon all believers beginning at Pentecost, the individual Christian became the new ark of the covenant—the temple within which God now chose for His Spirit—and His divine glory—to dwell.

❧

Now, back to the present.

We as a congregation are going to build a "house" for the Lord.[134] We don't use the word "temple" much anymore, but that's what we're talking about—a place where the Lord will cause His Spirit to dwell with us.

We have taken your suggestions and ideas and presented them to our architect. We are developing a design—a master plan for the Master's Place. We looked at the blueprints for Solomon's Temple, but don't think that model will get the job done for us. But we are making progress on the plan that will.

When the plan is approved, we will build it. And when the building is complete, it will be beautiful and inspiring. It will be everything we can afford to build for the Lord. We will be thrilled and will celebrate the new house of the Lord.

---

[132] Matthew 18:20, ESV.
[133] Ephesians 2:22, NIV.
[134] As it turned out, the local city council changed the zoning ordinance before we could begin construction, preventing us from bringing our plan to reality. We ended up purchasing a building in a better location from a congregation needing to downsize.

But it will be empty and useless, until God chooses to come into the house and fill it with His glory. And for God to come into our house as He did into Solomon's, there will have to be "a temple within the temple."

We will come into the house of the Lord to meet our gracious, loving God, but He will not be in our "house" unless He is first in our hearts. If we are not God's temple already—if God's Spirit has not already come to dwell within *us*—we will not find Him in a building, no matter how beautiful the building we build.

In ancient times, because God's holy words were kept securely sealed in the ark, God was willing to bless the ark and those who carried it and followed it with His abiding and almighty Presence. God was willing to meet His people, time after time and place after place, wherever the ark led them. And as long as the kings in Jerusalem and their subjects were willing to humble themselves in obedience before the laws of God, God would remain with them and dwell with them in the house Solomon built for Him.

The Psalmist said, *"I have hidden your word in my heart that I might not sin against you."*[135]

You are the temple within the temple. When you keep God's Word faithfully and obediently in your heart—when you make your life available to be the throne for God, the footstool of His divine glory—you will come into that new place we will build, with God in you, and around you in others. And God will fill that place and make it sacred, just as He has done with you.

God will have no interest in sending His Spirit to the building we will build unless we go there and gather together wanting with all our hearts to be, in the words of the Apostle Paul, *"joined together and ris[ing] to become a holy temple in the LORD…being built together to become that dwelling in which God lives by his Spirit."*[136]

We will build a building—a modern day temple—a house for the Lord—but only God can infuse the temple within the temple

---

[135] Psalm 119:11, NIV.
[136] Ephesians 2:21-22, NIV.

with the power and glory that will make it worthy to receive the almighty and infinite God. Only God can make you worthy to be the place in which He will cause His glory to dwell so that the house of the LORD where you pray and worship and study and serve and love will be filled with God as well.

There is a popular praise chorus whose words seem hauntingly relevant to this business of being the temple within the temple.

It goes like this:

> "Lord, prepare me
> to be a sanctuary,
> pure and holy,
> tried and true.
> With thanksgiving,
> I'll be a living
> sanctuary for you."[137]

In the weeks and months ahead, as we prepare for building the house of our Lord, pray that God will prepare you for when it will be completed, and you will come into that house to dwell with Him.

Have you thought what it will be like? Have you dreamed the dreams God would have you dream about the place where, because you are there, and God is in you and in all of us, God will set our church afire in glory and spiritual power?

The Psalmist has dreamed those dreams. Did you hear them as we read the Psalter together?

> *"One thing I ask from the Lord,*
> *this only do I seek:*
> *that I may dwell in the house of the Lord*
> *all the days of my life,*
> *to gaze on the beauty of the Lord*
> *and to seek him in his temple."*[138]

---

[137] Randy Scruggs and John Thompson, "Sanctuary," 1982.
[138] Psalm 27:4, NIV.

From 1st Kings 6 and 8

Imagine the house of the Lord, where He will
> *"hide [you] in the shelter of his tabernacle*
> *and set [you] high upon a rock..."*[139]
> *"where you will worship with joy;*
> *and sing and make music to the* LORD.*"*[140]

I will be glad when they say unto me:
> *"Let us go into the house of the Lord."*[141]

How about you?

❦

---

[139] Psalm 27:5, NIV.
[140] Psalm 27:6.
[141] Psalm 122:1, KJV.

From 1st Kings 19

1 Kings 19:1-8 ESV

¹ Ahab told Jezebel all that Elijah had done, and how he had killed all the prophets with the sword. ² Then Jezebel sent a messenger to Elijah, saying, "So may the gods do to me and more also, if I do not make your life as the life of one of them by this time tomorrow." ³ Then he was afraid, and he arose and ran for his life and came to Beersheba, which belongs to Judah, and left his servant there.

⁴ But he himself went a day's journey into the wilderness and came and sat down under a broom tree. And he asked that he might die, saying, "It is enough; now, O Lord, take away my life, for I am no better than my fathers." ⁵ And he lay down and slept under a broom tree. And behold, an angel touched him and said to him, "Arise and eat." ⁶ And he looked, and behold, there was at his head a cake baked on hot stones and a jar of water. And he ate and drank and lay down again. ⁷ And the angel of the Lord came again a second time and touched him and said, "Arise and eat, for the journey is too great for you." ⁸ And he arose and ate and drank, and went in the strength of that food forty days and forty nights to Horeb, the mount of God.

God's Food in the Desert

Matthew 4:1-11 ESV

¹ *Then Jesus was led up by the Spirit into the wilderness to be tempted by the devil.* ² *And after fasting forty days and forty nights, he was hungry.* ³ *And the tempter came and said to him, "If you are the Son of God, command these stones to become loaves of bread."*

⁴ *But he answered, "It is written,*

> *Man shall not live by bread alone,*
> *but by every word*
> *that comes from the mouth of God.'"*

⁵ *Then the devil took him to the holy city and set him on the pinnacle of the temple* ⁶ *and said to him, "If you are the Son of God, throw yourself down, for it is written,*

> *'He will command his angels concerning you,'*

and

> *'On their hands they will bear you up,*
> *lest you strike your foot against a stone.'"*

⁷ *Jesus said to him, "Again it is written,*

> *'You shall not put the Lord your God*
> *to the test.'"*

⁸ *Again, the devil took him to a very high mountain and showed him all the kingdoms of the world and their glory.* ⁹ *And he said to him, "All these I will give you, if you will fall down and worship me."*

¹⁰ *Then Jesus said to him, "Be gone, Satan! For it is written,*

> *'You shall worship the Lord your God*
> *and him only shall you serve.'"*

¹¹ *Then the devil left him, and behold, angels came and were ministering to him.*

16.

God's Food in the Desert

1 Kings 19:1-8; Matthew 4:1-11 ESV

Usually, when you win the Super Bowl, you go to Disney World. The contest between Elijah and the Baal Idolaters before a standing-room-only crowd at Mount Carmel was like a biblical Super Bowl. And Elijah, the most valuable—and only—player on God's side, won in a blow-out.

But he didn't go to Orlando after. That's understandable given that the losing side's leader put out a "contract" on him. If it sounds odd, just remember that it's the Bible, and as you may have noticed, they sometimes do things differently there.

Let's go to the replay: Elijah the prophet went and picked a fight with the ungodly king and queen of the country, and then challenged the hundreds of newly imported priests and prophets of the queen's god Baal to a sudden-death face-off to see which of these two gods really has the goods. Elijah's God came through like the Lord and Master of the universe He is, while Baal's boys lost game, set and *life*, right down to the last false prophet.

It was a great day for God, but Jezebel the queen isn't known for good sportsmanship, so before Elijah can run a victory lap, he has to run for his life. He does head south, but not for the thrills of a theme park. He hurries, not to Disney World, but south of the border (the border of Israel and Judah, that is), to the wilderness where, historically, God has been.

And as he goes, Elijah loses perspective. He loses his confidence, and then his hope, and then his will to live. Elijah comes right out and says it, "God, I've had enough! Just kill me and get it over with!"

Of course, he could have said the same thing to Jezebel before he took off and gotten his wish without wearing himself out. But, apparently, he only wanted God to do the deadly deed. Elijah won the battle against Baal at Mount Carmel (as God's agent, of course) and now, he's wandering out in the wilderness, disillusioned and despondent, waiting to die.

You know how he feels. The kings and queens of our country have done things in recent days that make us feel like we are the ones who got mauled at Mount Carmel. And then we hear powerful people telling us they're coming after us—Christian churches—if we continue to take God's side against theirs. These are depressing days—and dangerous. What's going on around us can break your heart and your spirit.

Or perhaps you're dealing with something more personal—some individual or family heartbreak or hazard that you can't see any way to overcome or avoid. And you just want to give up. Deep inside, something screams out, "Enough, Lord! I just can't do it anymore."

You've run as fast and as far as you can. You've walked on until you can't do that anymore, either. You just want to lie down and close your eyes and have it all be over. And like Elijah, that's what you do. You lie down, and you close your eyes and wait for "you don't know what"—helpless and hurting and hating how you feel.

☙❧

But look what happens to Elijah. Elijah hits bottom, but he doesn't die. He is touched by an angel. He wakes up from his

From 1st Kings 19

worries and his woes because God sends someone very special to wake him up. This is what God does. God lets Elijah rest—gives him rest—and then sends someone into Elijah's life to "touch" him—to change his life, or at least the way he looks at it.

God sends an angel to provide something that will strengthen Elijah and encourage him. It isn't a lot, really—a little bread and something to drink. But there it is, when it wasn't there before—or Elijah hadn't noticed it, in his depressed state of mind.

And it's enough.

God provides for Elijah, through the angel, who wakes Elijah up from his despair and shows him how things are better than he thought they were. And because the angel is there with him—while he is sleeping and when he has awakened—Elijah is not alone in his darkest moment, because God doesn't want him to be—and makes sure that he isn't.

Again, this is what God does.

Of course, God doesn't snap His divine fingers—or the angel his angelic ones—and make every problem disappear for Elijah.

That's *not* what God does.

Elijah wakes up to the angel's touch and does as the angel tells him. He eats and drinks and goes back to sleep.

And while Elijah sleeps, what is the angel doing?

He's protecting Elijah. He's guarding him from all the natural and supernatural dangers that would attack him if God did not send His angel to watch over him and minister to him in his need.

~~~

And then, for Elijah as for us, the process is repeated. The angel touches him again, and wakes him up again, and tells him again to take the nourishment God has provided for him—and this time, the angel tells Elijah something else—something more: You have to take and eat what the Lord provides for you because without it, the journey—what lies ahead for you—will be too hard for you.

You see, when you think you've come to the end of your rope—it's not the end. When you think, "That's it!"—it isn't. God has more planned for you.

But you can't do it on your own. You can't get there under your own steam. You didn't even get where you are now under your own steam. God has been sending angels to wake you up and feed you and encourage you all your life.

Sometimes they might be the "you-can't-see'em—heavenly forever and ever" kind. Mostly, I suspect, they're the temporarily deputized and especially spiritually empowered, average old earthly kind—which means that most of us have probably been angels from time to time, without knowing it, sent by God to touch somebody and nourish that somebody a little bit with whatever God gave us for the purpose.

It's kind of nice to think of having been somebody's angel some time—and that you might be somebody's angel again, if it suites God's purpose to use you that way.

※

I said God has more planned.

Elijah, for instance, thinks he is on his way to the morgue. He's actually on his way to Mount Sinai for an encounter with God even more amazing than what he and everybody else experienced with God on Mount Carmel. On the holy mountain, where God revealed His glory to Moses in smoke and thunder, God will speak to Elijah—in silence itself. Wherever you are in your life, you are on your way to a personal and powerful encounter with God in a place that He has made holy.

But the "going" often does beat you down and wear you out.

Can you make it through what you're going through?

Maybe you don't know. So this morning, remember: God provides something that will strengthen and encourage you in your hardest times. It isn't a lot, really—a little bread and something to drink. But there it is. And it will be enough. This is what God does.

From 1st Kings 19

And this time, God hasn't sent an angel to provide it for you. He has sent His only-begotten Son, Who spent His own difficult days in the desert—hungry, tired and tempted—before God sent angels to minister to Him. Jesus is the One Who says to you today, "Arise and eat."

And He is the One Who will nourish you so that you can make it through everything you're going through—on this journey to that holy place with God.

"Arise and eat."[142]

---

[142] This sermon was followed by the serving of communion.

From the Book of 2nd Kings

2 Kings 5:1-15 ESV

¹ *Naaman, commander of the army of the king of Syria, was a great man with his master and in high favor, because by him the* LORD *had given victory to Syria. He was a mighty man of valor, but he was a leper.* ² *Now the Syrians on one of their raids had carried off a little girl from the land of Israel, and she worked in the service of Naaman's wife.* ³ *She said to her mistress, "Would that my lord were with the prophet who is in Samaria! He would cure him of his leprosy."* ⁴ *So Naaman went in and told his lord, "Thus and so spoke the girl from the land of Israel."* ⁵ *And the king of Syria said, "Go now, and I will send a letter to the king of Israel."*

So he went, taking with him ten talents of silver, six thousand shekels of gold, and ten changes of clothing. ⁶ *And he brought the letter to the king of Israel, which read, "When this letter reaches you, know that I have sent to you Naaman my servant, that you may cure him of his leprosy."* ⁷ *And when the king of Israel read the letter, he tore his clothes and said, "Am I God, to kill and to make alive, that this man sends word to me to cure a man of his leprosy? Only consider, and see how he is seeking a quarrel with me."*

⁸ *But when Elisha the man of God heard that the king of Israel had torn his clothes, he sent to the king, saying, "Why have you torn your clothes? Let him come now to me, that he may know that there is a prophet in Israel."* ⁹ *So Naaman came with his horses and chariots and stood at the door of Elisha's house.* ¹⁰ *And Elisha sent a messenger to him, saying, "Go and wash in the Jordan seven times, and your flesh shall be restored, and you shall be clean."* ¹¹ *But Naaman was angry and went away, saying, "Behold, I thought that he would surely come out to me and stand and call upon the name of the* LORD *his God, and wave his hand over the place and cure the leper.* ¹² *Are not Abana and Pharpar, the rivers of Damascus, better than all the waters of Israel? Could I not wash in them and be clean?" So he turned and went away in a rage.* ¹³ *But his servants came near and said to him, "My father, it is a great word the prophet has spoken to you; will you not do it? Has he actually said to you, 'Wash, and be clean'?"* ¹⁴ *So he went down and dipped himself seven times in the Jordan, according to the word of the man of God, and his flesh was restored like the flesh of a little child, and he was clean.*

Things That Kings Can't Do

¹⁵ *Then he returned to the man of God, he and all his company, and he came and stood before him. And he said, "Behold, I know that there is no God in all the earth but in Israel...."*

17.

Things That Kings Can't Do

2 Kings 5:1-15 ESV

Where do you go when you need a miracle?

One option, apparently, is to turn to the government. The king of Syria sent his head soldier, Naaman, to the king of Israel with a note that said, "With this letter, I am sending my servant Naaman to you, so that you may cure him of his leprosy."

Of course, the Syrians don't expect something for nothing—even though they were more or less calling the shots in Israel about this time. No, the king of Syria knows how governments work and so he sent a little "foreign aid" along to compensate his counterpart for his time and trouble. "I hear there's a miracle worker in Israel," says the foreign king, "and I assume it's you, the guy heading up the government. After all, government is where all the power is."

But here's the funny thing: the king of Israel doesn't do miracles. He's head of the government—head of the country—but healing leprosy is not part of his portfolio. There is no department, agency or office in his administration taking care of miracles. The king doesn't make the rain fall. He doesn't make the crops grow. He can't stop the locust from wiping out the crops that do grow. He can't cure incurable diseases—like leprosy. But there sits

Naaman, out in the royal waiting room—waiting to be healed—waiting for his miracle.

And inside—in the throne room—in the inner sanctum where the political leader of the people of God reigns—panic reigns instead. How can you say "no" to the Syrians? And yet, everybody in the room, the king and all his key advisors, know something that the other king and his military commander apparently do not: There are things that kings can't do.

❧

And that reality hasn't changed.

It was true in ancient Israel. It has been true in every country around the world and throughout every generation in history. Today, kings have become figureheads or have given way to presidents and prime ministers. Governments have become more sophisticated in form and more ambitious in function. But the truth does not change: There are things that kings—and governments—cannot do.

Kings and governments do not do the kind of miracles that require the kind of power God has reserved to Himself. And the king of Israel is wise enough to know the difference: "Am *I—God?!*"

Not everyone who seeks or possesses power is as wise. And not everyone who desperately wants a miracle is as discerning, either. We find it very hard to make the distinction between the accumulation of human power and the possession of divine power, even when we could. Like Naaman, we can spend our lives in the waiting rooms of inadequate power, convincing ourselves that we have come to the place where miracles are to be found, only to waste our time and our lives.

"I need a miracle!"

"Don't we all, brother? But this is not the place. We're just the government."

From 2nd Kings 5

The king of Israel knew there was a God—and that it wasn't him or his government.

We can give him credit for that. It's more than the Syrians knew.

But does the king of Israel not know where to go when you need a miracle?

Apparently not.

And how wrong is that?! Even a little Israelite girl captured and carried into slavery in a foreign country knows where you go when you need a miracle: *"If only my master would see the prophet who is in Samaria! He would cure him of his leprosy."*

God didn't put His power in the palace; He put it in the person of the prophet Elisha.

And when Elisha heard that Naaman had gone to the king for his cure (word travels fast in capital cities, apparently) he sent for the poor fellow.

Now, I don't think Elisha was all that concerned to get the king off the hook. Elisha sent for Naaman because he knew where Naaman needed to go for that miracle he needed.

We tend to think of prophets as people who foretell the future or put the present in its proper, spiritual perspective. But Elisha—and his mentor, Elijah—were also men so full of the Spirit of God that God performed miracles through them. Elisha was going to heal Naaman of his leprosy for the same reason that Jesus would heal lepers in the New Testament:[143] so that those who did not know God would encounter Him in the miracle and have their lives changed forever.

So Naaman, who went to a king looking for a miracle, was sent to a man of God—where he found that miracle he was looking for.

ಶ್ರೀ

Where do *you* go when you need a miracle?

---

[143] Matthew 8:1-3; Luke 17:11-19.

You should go to God. And the best way to do that may be to go to Someone in Whom the Spirit of God dwells with power. Paul wrote to the Colossians that *"in him all the fullness of God was pleased to dwell."*[144] And we have come to Christ for the miracle of redemption and salvation and grace. Paul wrote to the Ephesians, *"I pray that...Christ may dwell in your hearts through faith...and that you may be filled to the measure of all the fullness of God."*[145]

And so now we, the forgiven, redeemed and regenerated people of God, are to be the people to whom others may come to discover the power of God, because God has caused His power to dwell in us. You know people need miracles in their lives; you've needed your own from time to time. And we know where to send them for the miracle power of God.

But what do you do when you need a miracle?

Elisha's house wasn't where Naaman thought he was going to find his healing miracle, much less the Jordan River where Elisha sent word for him to go. Naaman was highly offended by what Elisha told him to do to be healed. But the truth is that if you have to go to God to get the miracle you need, you will also have to do what God tells you to do if you are going to make the miracle God wants and waits to do for you your own.

There are things that kings can't do. And there are ways that simply will not work. You cannot get from God what you can only get from God if you are determined to get it *your* way. You must get your miracle God's way, or you will not get it at all.

※

Naaman was a mighty warrior. He had defeated many enemies, but he could not defeat leprosy. Naaman was a man of power and position where he came from, the king's right-hand man, but to get the miracle he wanted—and needed—he had to go to another place, and humble himself to the point of powerless obedience to

---

[144] Colossians 1:19, NIV.
[145] Ephesians 3:16-19, NIV.

a command that made no sense according to his worldly way of thinking, though it would ultimately make all the difference in the world.

And that is what we do to experience the miracles of God—the miracle of help—the miracle of hope—the miracle of healing: *Go to God and do His will.*

Have you noticed that when Naaman finally did what Elisha told him to do and was healed, he didn't come back to Elisha to show off his healing, but to proclaim the God he had discovered—encountered—in the process? More important than our miracles is the God we meet in receiving them. More important than our miracles are the miracles God performs through us to draw others to Himself.

There are things that kings can't do.

But God is different. God is in the miracle business. And because He is—and because we're His church—we, like Elisha, are in the miracle business, too.

Holy Housecleaning

2 Kings 22:1 – 23:3 ESV

22 ¹ *Josiah was eight years old when he began to reign, and he reigned thirty-one years in Jerusalem. His mother's name was Jedidah the daughter of Adaiah of Bozkath.* ² *And he did what was right in the eyes of the* LORD *and walked in all the way of David his father, and he did not turn aside to the right or to the left.*

³ *In the eighteenth year of King Josiah, the king sent Shaphan the son of Azaliah, son of Meshullam, the secretary, to the house of the* LORD, *saying,* ⁴ *"Go up to Hilkiah the high priest, that he may count the money that has been brought into the house of the* LORD, *which the keepers of the threshold have collected from the people.* ⁵ *And let it be given into the hand of the workmen who have the oversight of the house of the* LORD, *and let them give it to the workmen who are at the house of the* LORD, *repairing the house* ⁶ *(that is, to the carpenters, and to the builders, and to the masons), and let them use it for buying timber and quarried stone to repair the house.* ⁷ *But no accounting shall be asked from them for the money that is delivered into their hand, for they deal honestly."* ⁸ *And Hilkiah the high priest said to Shaphan the secretary, "I have found the Book of the Law in the house of the* LORD." *And Hilkiah gave the book to Shaphan, and he read it.* ⁹ *And Shaphan the secretary came to the king, and reported to the king, "Your servants have emptied out the money that was found in the house and have delivered it into the hand of the workmen who have the oversight of the house of the* LORD." ¹⁰ *Then Shaphan the secretary told the king, "Hilkiah the priest has given me a book." And Shaphan read it before the king.*

¹¹ *When the king heard the words of the Book of the Law, he tore his clothes.* ¹² *And the king commanded Hilkiah the priest, and Ahikam the son of Shaphan, and Achbor the son of Micaiah, and Shaphan the secretary, and Asaiah the king's servant, saying,* ¹³ *"Go, inquire of the* LORD *for me, and for the people, and for all Judah, concerning the words of this book that has been found. For great is the wrath of the* LORD *that is kindled against us, because our fathers have not obeyed the words of this book, to do according to all that is written concerning us."*

From 2nd Kings 22 and 23

¹⁴ So Hilkiah the priest, and Ahikam, and Achbor, and Shaphan, and Asaiah went to Huldah the prophetess, the wife of Shallum the son of Tikvah, son of Harhas, keeper of the wardrobe (now she lived in Jerusalem in the Second Quarter), and they talked with her. ¹⁵ And she said to them, "Thus says the LORD, *the God of Israel: 'Tell the man who sent you to me, ¹⁶ Thus says the* LORD, *Behold, I will bring disaster upon this place and upon its inhabitants, all the words of the book that the king of Judah has read. ¹⁷ Because they have forsaken me and have made offerings to other gods, that they might provoke me to anger with all the work of their hands, therefore my wrath will be kindled against this place, and it will not be quenched. ¹⁸ But to the king of Judah, who sent you to inquire of the* LORD, *thus shall you say to him, Thus says the* LORD, *the God of Israel: Regarding the words that you have heard, ¹⁹ because your heart was penitent, and you humbled yourself before the* LORD, *when you heard how I spoke against this place and against its inhabitants, that they should become a desolation and a curse, and you have torn your clothes and wept before me, I also have heard you, declares the* LORD. *²⁰ Therefore, behold, I will gather you to your fathers, and you shall be gathered to your grave in peace, and your eyes shall not see all the disaster that I will bring upon this place.'" And they brought back word to the king.*

23 *¹ Then the king sent, and all the elders of Judah and Jerusalem were gathered to him. ² And the king went up to the house of the* LORD, *and with him all the men of Judah and all the inhabitants of Jerusalem and the priests and the prophets, all the people, both small and great. And he read in their hearing all the words of the Book of the Covenant that had been found in the house of the* LORD. *³ And the king stood by the pillar and made a covenant before the* LORD, *to walk after the* LORD *and to keep his commandments and his testimonies and his statutes with all his heart and all his soul, to perform the words of this covenant that were written in this book. And all the people joined in the covenant.*

Holy Housecleaning

John 2:13-22 ESV

[13] The Passover of the Jews was at hand, and Jesus went up to Jerusalem. [14] In the temple he found those who were selling oxen and sheep and pigeons, and the money-changers sitting there. [15] And making a whip of cords, he drove them all out of the temple, with the sheep and oxen. And he poured out the coins of the money-changers and overturned their tables. [16] And he told those who sold the pigeons, "Take these things away; do not make my Father's house a house of trade." [17] His disciples remembered that it was written, "Zeal for your house will consume me."

[18] So the Jews said to him, "What sign do you show us for doing these things?" [19] Jesus answered them, "Destroy this temple, and in three days I will raise it up." [20] The Jews then said, "It has taken forty-six years to build this temple, and will you raise it up in three days?" [21] But he was speaking about the temple of his body. [22] When therefore he was raised from the dead, his disciples remembered that he had said this, and they believed the Scripture and the word that Jesus had spoken.

18.

Holy Housecleaning

2 Kings 22:1 – 23:3; John 2:13-22 ESV

Last week, you heard that *"in the year that King Uzziah died,"* Isaiah *"saw the LORD, high and lifted up."*[146] Now, a century has passed—a hundred years since the prophet saw the glory of God filling the Temple Solomon built in Jerusalem.

In that time, other kings came and went—as did priests and prophets. As year gave way to year, the people in power had increasingly focused on other things—like important matters of state—because they were living in hard and dangerous times. Conditions called for constant and careful attention to the art and craft of politics so that foreign powers would be kept at bay.

And while the powerful people in Jerusalem devoted themselves to the exercise of power, the place in Jerusalem where the greatest Power of all had chosen for His Presence to dwell ceased to be central to the life of the nation or the policies of the state. The people of God had gradually come to ignore the God Who had made them His people.

And ignoring God, they naturally neglected His holy house. The people did not attend upon God as they were supposed to.

---

[146] Isaiah 6:1, RSV.

Holy Housecleaning

They did not *"come into his presence with singing"* as they should have. They did not *"enter his gates with thanksgiving"* or *"his courts with praise."*[147] They did not bring their tithes and offerings as frequently or fully as they had been directed to do.[148] Because they did not come into the Temple, they were not there to bless God's Name. They did not seek out God's Word—to read it—to study it—to learn it—to know it—to obey it.

And the house where heaven would come down to earth and glow with a divine glory upon walls erected by human hands was left to gather dust and fill up with clutter and suffer the indignity of indifference and disregard.

Were they too busy with domestic politics and foreign policy to attend to the One Who raises up and brings down nations[149]— the One Who chose them out of all the people of the world to be His treasured possession[150]—the One Who said, *"I have consecrated this temple...by putting my name there forever...my eyes and my heart will always be there..."*?[151]

❧

Whatever the reason, there He waited—for a nation that did not come.

Oh, it wasn't that they had stopped being religious. The kings and their courts may have become distracted by affairs of state, but not the people across the land. They were distracted by something else. They were distracted from the Temple by religion itself. There was a lot of competition around the country for the country's religious business—for their attention, attendance and allegiance.

Other temples were up and running in other cities. Other shrines and altars stood atop any number of high places, attracting

---

[147] Psalm 100:2, 4, KJV.
[148] Deuteronomy 12:11.
[149] Job 12:23.
[150] Deuteronomy 7:6.
[151] 1 Kings 9:3, NIV.

From 2nd Kings 22 and 23

local interest. Other sites around the countryside claimed to be holy—and a whole lot more convenient for discharging your religious duties than carting yourself and your sacrifice down the road and up the hill all the way to Jerusalem, so many miles away.

But all these other religious operations were distractions because even those places that claimed to worship God weren't always careful to avoid "adjustments"—in their theology and morality—to accommodate local attitudes and preferences. And there were just as many places that didn't even pretend to worship the God of Israel. The "foreign god franchises" were running a brisk business because there are always people who really don't care who or what they worship as long as they are having a good time while they're doing it. And even back then, there were plenty of religions whose whole point seemed to be: Have a good time.

And then one day, the head of state decided to turn his attention to the Temple next door. Josiah became king when he was eight years old. Unlike his father and grandfather before him, Josiah *"did what was right in the eyes of the LORD."* When he grew up, he ordered the destruction of the distractions to the proper worship of God. Throughout his kingdom, and as far beyond it as his authority would reach, Josiah tore down and burned up any place that competed with the Temple as the place where God's people were to meet Him.

And in Jerusalem, Josiah reversed the results of years of neglect and indifference on the house of God. He ordered the Temple restored to its former glory so that the infinitely greater glory of God, formerly found there, would be willing to appear there again. Josiah attended to the Temple because he was attending to God.

And then a funny thing happened. Make that: a "marvelous, miraculous" thing. In the process of restoring the house of God, the king's people rediscovered the Word of God—the blueprint for a healthy, happy and holy society.

It makes you wonder: Which did they start neglecting first? Would God's people have ever neglected His house if they had not first neglected His Word?

On the other hand, if they had not neglected God's house, could they ever have forgotten or misplaced God's Word?

The restoration of the Temple continued, but now, because of what he read in God's Word, the king knew another kind of restoration was necessary. Now the people and the nation had to be restored in their relationship with the God Who had called them into being and committed Himself to living in loving covenant with them. So, the carpenters and the builders and the stonemasons went on with their work in the Temple while the king went to work on the other matter.

The Bible says Josiah rent his clothes and repented for the sins of the nation he led. He called the whole kingdom to repentance. He went up to the Temple, and led the leaders of God's people he had commanded to come with him. Their king *"read in their hearing all the words of the book of the covenant that had been found in the house of the LORD."* And by finding the book and reading the words, they found, as well, the covenant with God they had misplaced.

The Temple was restored by the dedication and work of the people who took up the task.

And the people were restored by the dedication and work of God Who, despite their neglect and distraction, took up the divine task of their redemption.

ॐ

This week, we selected the architects who will design the structure that will become our house of God. We have marked the site where it will rise toward heaven. In time—and soon, we hope—workmen will begin raising the walls of the place where God will cause His glory to dwell.

There, as here, we will enter with hearts full of thanksgiving and lips singing God's praise.

And there, as here, we will find the Word of God, but not because we stumble across it in a neglected sanctuary. We will find it because we will seek it in the place where we know we will meet our God, knowing as well that by seeking His Word we will find it and the message God would reveal to us in it.

And, like Josiah, we will call all those who have neglected their faith or been distracted by a distorted or competing gospel to join us. And we will lead them into a place where God's Word is faithfully proclaimed, and His grace is humbly sought, and His glory is powerfully revealed, so that they, too, may join in the covenant God offers freely through the shed blood of another King—a greater King—Who, even more than Josiah, *"did what was right in the eyes of the LORD."*

King Jesus did some holy housecleaning of His own in the Temple in Jerusalem, according to the Gospels. And when He was criticized for doing so, He told His accusers, *"Destroy this temple, and I will raise it again in three days."*

And destroy it they did, eagerly, because they had neglected the deeper things of God so long that they could not recognize God's Word-made-flesh[152] even when He walked and talked among them in the Temple of their day.

Josiah the king repaired a temple that had been neglected for years by an indifferent people of God. Jesus *replaced* their temple with another One, a temple not made with human hands, a temple to which we all may go and know that, by the grace of God, in *this* temple, it is we who have been restored.

---

[152] John 1:14.

From the Book of Esther

From Esther 4

Esther 4:6-16 ESV

⁶ Hathach went out to Mordecai in the open square of the city in front of the king's gate, ⁷ and Mordecai told him all that had happened to him, and the exact sum of money that Haman had promised to pay into the king's treasuries for the destruction of the Jews. ⁸ Mordecai also gave him a copy of the written decree issued in Susa for their destruction, that he might show it to Esther and explain it to her and command her to go to the king to beg his favor and plead with him on behalf of her people. ⁹ And Hathach went and told Esther what Mordecai had said. ¹⁰ Then Esther spoke to Hathach and commanded him to go to Mordecai and say, ¹¹ "All the king's servants and the people of the king's provinces know that if any man or woman goes to the king inside the inner court without being called, there is but one law—to be put to death, except the one to whom the king holds out the golden scepter so that he may live. But as for me, I have not been called to come in to the king these thirty days."

¹² And they told Mordecai what Esther had said. ¹³ Then Mordecai told them to reply to Esther, "Do not think to yourself that in the king's palace you will escape any more than all the other Jews. ¹⁴ For if you keep silent at this time, relief and deliverance will rise for the Jews from another place, but you and your father's house will perish. And who knows whether you have not come to the kingdom for such a time as this?" ¹⁵ Then Esther told them to reply to Mordecai, ¹⁶ "Go, gather all the Jews to be found in Susa, and hold a fast on my behalf, and do not eat or drink for three days, night or day. I and my young women will also fast as you do. Then I will go to the king, though it is against the law, and if I perish, I perish."

John 18:28-37 ESV

²⁸ Then they led Jesus from the house of Caiaphas to the governor's headquarters. It was early morning. They themselves did not enter the governor's headquarters, so that they would not be defiled, but could eat the Passover. ²⁹ So Pilate went outside to them and said, "What accusation do you bring against this man?" ³⁰ They answered him, "If this man were not doing evil, we would not have delivered him over to you." ³¹ Pilate said to them, "Take him yourselves and judge him by your own law." The Jews said to him, "It is not lawful for us to put anyone to death." ³² This was to fulfill the word that Jesus had spoken to show by what kind of death he was going to die.

³³ So Pilate entered his headquarters again and called Jesus and said to him, "Are you the King of the Jews?" ³⁴ Jesus answered, "Do you say this of your own accord, or did others say it to you about me?" ³⁵ Pilate answered, "Am I a Jew? Your own nation and the chief priests have delivered you over to me. What have you done?" ³⁶ Jesus answered, "My kingdom is not of this world. If my kingdom were of this world, my servants would have been fighting, that I might not be delivered over to the Jews. But my kingdom is not from the world." ³⁷ Then Pilate said to him, "So you are a king?" Jesus answered, "You say that I am a king. For this purpose I was born and for this purpose I have come into the world—to bear witness to the truth. Everyone who is of the truth listens to my voice."

19.

For Such a Time As This

Esther 4:6-16; John 18:28-37 ESV

Usually, when you think of spiritual gifts, you think of things like piety or prophecy. Breath-taking beauty is not what usually comes to mind. But it seems that being drop-dead gorgeous was Esther's spiritual gift. That's what God gave her so she would be in the right place when it came time to do God's will.

It's not the most familiar story, so let me summarize: A Persian queen embarrasses and angers a Persian king when she refuses his command to come and "strut her stuff" in front of a bunch of drunken soldiers and civil servants. The king then has to "fire" the queen so all the other wives in the empire don't get the idea they can treat their husbands the same way, which means there's now a vacancy for the position of queen of the empire.

To fill the vacancy, the king is encouraged to check out all the good-looking girls in his kingdom before choosing one to wear the crown. In truth, the king doesn't require a lot of encouragement. He quickly approves a program in which hundreds of beautiful girls are brought to the capital to spend a year soaking in the imperial spa and sampling all the costliest cosmetics in preparation for the preliminary competition. Those who make it through the preliminaries go on to the bonus round, where the decision of the judge—the king himself—is final.

In the end, the king picks a girl named Esther. Esther moves into the queen's quarters and the king moves on to other things.

Esther, as it happens, is Jewish, though the king doesn't know that yet. Neither does a guy named Haman, who hates the Jews because he hates Esther's cousin, a guy named Mordecai, who hates Haman back just as much.

Haman hatches a plot to wipe out Mordecai and the Jews, but Mordecai hears about it and has a fit. He figures the only person who can put a stop to the slaughter is the king, and the only person who can get the king to do that is Esther, the queen—the Jewish queen.

Mordecai puts the problem to Esther, but when he does, she points out a problem in Mordecai's plan. If Esther goes to see the king and the king doesn't want to see her, she won't have to wait for Haman's henchmen to come kill her. The king will have her killed on the spot, which won't help the Jews at all—or her, either, for that matter.

Mordecai mentions the fact that if she doesn't go to the king, being queen won't save her from Haman, and that her becoming queen may have been for the very purpose of saving her people from this plot. Esther accepts the logic of Mordecai's argument and goes to the king, who does not have her killed, which is crucial if the story is to continue, which it does.

By this time, Haman is the king's right-hand man and Esther very carefully sets the stage for turning the tables on him with the king. After stringing the process out for days, she finally lays the whole story out for the king, who strings Haman up in minutes, hanging him and all his sons on the gallows Haman had built for hanging Mordecai.

Esther survives. The Jews survive. Mordecai survives—and takes Haman's place as the king's prime minister. And the Jews get a holiday out of the whole thing. End of story.

Now that you know the story, let's get to the point.

It's not the romance. It's not the intrigue. It's not the adventure. The point of the story is that there was a purpose in what happened to Esther—a divine purpose. She didn't know about it ahead of time. She wasn't sure about it *at* the time.

But she had to look at her life and consider that where she had been, and where she was, were not meaningless accidents or irrelevant details in a life that had no greater purpose. Mordecai forced her to face the question: "Why have these things happened to me?"

It is not unusual to ask that question when the things that are happening to you are painful, or scary, or disappointing. Your health fails, or you lose a loved one: "Why me!?" Troubles mount up and your coping skills falter: "Why, Lord!?" You look around and see the moral meltdown of what used to be a world that was so much better and brighter, safer and saner, and you wonder in disbelief and despair, "Why are these things happening? Why is *this* my life right now?"

"Why!?"—which really means, "Why don't You get me out of this, God? Why don't You stop the pain? Why don't You take away the hardship or stress or danger? Why don't You make it better?"

God does that, of course. He makes all things better. *"In all things, God works for the good...."*[153] But a lot of times, He doesn't stop the pain or take away the thing you fear or struggle with—which invites you to ask again, and differently: "Why?"

What is the reason that God has put you in, or at least *allowed* you to be in, the situation in life where you find yourself? Is there a reason?

⁂

Those who do not believe in God, or that there is a God, will tell you there *is* no reason for your life, or for any part of it. You

---

[153] Romans 8:28, NIV.

and everything about you—and everything about this world you live in—are all accidents. Everything is random and meaningless in the grand scheme of things because there is no grand scheme of things. There is just what happens.

There is no reason for suffering, or struggling, or putting up with the unpleasant things in life. You're just stuck with what you've got, unless you can find or figure out a way to get out of it, which you should, because there's no point in putting up with what you don't like if you don't have to.

Doing what you want is the only "reason" in life—"they" say.

But if there is a God, a God Who happens to be—as we professed earlier—our "Father Almighty" and "Maker of heaven and earth, and of all things visible and invisible,"[154] then it is reasonable to assume—and to believe the Bible when it tells you—that you were made, and are being "parented," with a divine and benevolent purpose in mind—in *God's* Mind.

And in every moment of your life—in everything you experience—there is a divine purpose—there is something that God wants you to do with what you've got—what life has dealt you.

This is true of the hard parts of life—those that I mentioned a moment ago, and so many others you have gone through and are going through that I haven't mentioned. God has a purpose for you're being there—or here.

But this is also true of the other times—the good times when what's happening is wonderful, pleasing, enriching. God also has a purpose for those times in your life. You're not inclined so much to ask the "Why?" question then, but you should.

---

[154] From "The Nicene Creed," *The Episcopal Book of Common Prayer*, 1928.

From Esther 4

Esther was made a queen. She had it made. She was on top of the world. "Don't look a gift horse in the mouth—just take it and ride it as far as it will take you!"

But Mordecai says, "Put it all on the line—the whole 'queen thing'—and your life to boot—because that may be the very reason why God put you there."

Good or bad—whatever you're going through—God has a purpose for it—a reason for your being where you are. You may not be able to see that God has a reason—much less what that reason is. Esther had trouble with the concept at first. Mordecai had to help her see it.

☙❧

But there was Another Who understood the business of God's purpose for our lives even better than Mordecai. Standing before Pilate—staring His own death squarely in the face—Jesus told the man about to pass judgment on Him, *"…for this reason I was born, and for this I came into the world…."*

Jesus was fulfilling the purpose of His whole life by passing through that judgment hall on the way to the Cross, which was the only way to save His people from the destruction that awaited them.

Before that, when Jesus still had the freedom to save Himself from the purpose of His life, He told a crowd, *"The hour has come for the Son of man to be glorified…. He who loves his life loses it, and he who hates his life in this world will keep it for eternal life…. Now is my soul troubled. And what shall I say? 'Father, save me from this hour'? No, for this purpose I have come to this hour."*[155]

Paul picked up the idea in Romans: *"If we live, we live to the Lord; and if we die, we die to the Lord. So then, whether we live or whether we die, we are the Lord's. For to this end, Christ died and lived again, that he might be Lord both of the dead and of the living."*[156]

---

[155] John 12:23, 25, 27, RSV.
[156] Romans 14:8-9, RSV.

"For this reason...."

You exist for a divine purpose. There is a purpose waiting to be discovered and embraced in every circumstance in your life—every difficulty—every blessing. God's purpose in your circumstances may be obvious. Probably—usually—it will not be.

But consider how your life will change—how its meaning will deepen—when the question you ask is not "God, why don't You get me out of this mess?" or "How can I get the most out of this good time?", but "Lord, what do You want me to do in this situation? What is Your reason for this?"

Why are you living in this time in history–in this country? Why are you in this community–in this church–in this service? Why do you have the strengths, abilities and personality you have? And why—for God's purposes—do you have your weaknesses? What does God in His infinite wisdom and love want of you and for you right now, given what's going on in your life?

God made Esther a queen so she could do His will—and risk her life in the process. God sent Jesus to the Cross so He could do God's will—and give up His life in the process.[157] God has put you where you are, not so you will suffer—or celebrate—but so that you will be able to do His will for you.

Ask the question.
Discover His reason.
Do His will.

---

[157] 1 John 4:9.

From the Book of Job

Job 40:1-14 ESV

¹ And the L*ORD said to Job:*
² "Shall a faultfinder contend with the Almighty?
He who argues with God, let him answer it."
³ Then Job answered the L*ORD and said:*
⁴ "Behold, I am of small account; what shall I answer you?
I lay my hand on my mouth.
⁵ I have spoken once, and I will not answer;
twice, but I will proceed no further."
⁶ Then the L*ORD answered Job out of the whirlwind and said:*
⁷ "Dress for action like a man;
I will question you, and you make it known to me.
⁸ Will you even put me in the wrong?
Will you condemn me that you may be in the right?
⁹ Have you an arm like God,
and can you thunder with a voice like his?
¹⁰ Adorn yourself with majesty and dignity;
clothe yourself with glory and splendor.
¹¹ Pour out the overflowings of your anger,
and look on everyone who is proud and abase him.
¹² Look on everyone who is proud and bring him low
and tread down the wicked where they stand.
¹³ Hide them all in the dust together;
bind their faces in the world below.
¹⁴ Then will I also acknowledge to you
that your own right hand can save you."

ಈ–ಲ

Revelation 4:2-11 ESV

²At once I was in the Spirit, and behold, a throne stood in heaven, with one seated on the throne. ³And he who sat there had the appearance of jasper and carnelian, and around the throne was a rainbow that had the appearance of an emerald. ⁴Around the throne were twenty-four thrones, and seated on the thrones were twenty-four elders, clothed in white garments, with golden crowns on their heads. ⁵From the throne came flashes of lightning, and rumblings and peals of thunder, and before the throne were burning seven torches of fire, which are the seven spirits of God, ⁶and before the throne there was as it were a sea of glass, like crystal.

And around the throne, on each side of the throne, are four living creatures, full of eyes in front and behind: ⁷the first living creature like a lion, the second living creature like an ox, the third living creature with the face of a man, and the fourth living creature like an eagle in flight. ⁸And the four living creatures, each of them with six wings, are full of eyes all around and within, and day and night they never cease to say,

"Holy, holy, holy, is the Lord God Almighty,
who was and is and is to come!"

⁹And whenever the living creatures give glory and honor and thanks to him who is seated on the throne, who lives forever and ever, ¹⁰the twenty-four elders fall down before him who is seated on the throne and worship him who lives forever and ever. They cast their crowns before the throne, saying,

¹¹"Worthy are you, our Lord and God,
to receive glory and honor and power,
for you created all things,
and by your will they existed and were created."

20.

Who Died and Made You God?

Job 40:1-14; Revelation 4:2-11 ESV

"Who died and made you God?!"

It's an odd title for a sermon, I grant you, and you may have found it offensive when you read it. It is intended to be offensive.

It's one of those playground taunts that children like to serve up to someone who's acting too high and mighty for their liking—somebody who's trying to take over the process and call the shots and break the rules, or at least bend then to their own advantage. Nobody knows where the expression came from, but everybody has probably used it—or wanted to—some time or other.

Basically, it is the question put to Job in the passage we heard earlier this morning, though not in so many words. After an avalanche of adversity had crashed down on Job—after his so-called friends had bombarded him with the worst excuse for consolation the world has ever seen—after his own agonizing effort to make sense of his suffering had fallen far short of satisfaction—Job got the visit from God he had been demanding.

And what did God say?

That's right: "Who died and made you God?"

Why would God challenge Job this way, after all Job had been through—after all that God had knowingly allowed Job to go through?

Could it be that Job—consciously or unconsciously—had come to the conclusion that he could—or would—do a better job than God had at running the world that had run amok for him?

For almost 40 chapters, Job had defended his innocence against all accusations. He had demanded justice over and over from the God Who, alone, could give it to him. And God's answer, in the end, is simply, "Let's be clear about which one of us is God."

~~~

And God could say the same thing to many in our world today—for many in our modern world have decided that God has died—or simply does not exist—which means that anybody who wants to can be God. This is the thrust of the growing secular mindset in our culture. Though Christians have pushed back on this perspective—see, for instance, the recent movie, "God's Not Dead,"[158]—the mindset that more and more have assumed—that God does not exist—is an outgrowth of ideas put forward in the 1960s by radical theologians, and picked up by popular media like *TIME* magazine that asked on an ominous cover in 1966, "Is God Dead?"[159]

Those who asked the question assumed the answer to be "yes." And that possibility became popular with people who did not want to be constrained by a code of right and wrong established (and, therefore, enforced) by a supreme Authority Whose will could not be contested.

The sense is that, "if there is no God, all things are permissible,"—an idea attributed to several famous authors, including C. S. Lewis.[160]

---

[158] *God's Not Dead,* Pure Flix Entertainment, 2014.
[159] "Is God Dead?" *TIME*, April 8, 1965.
[160] C. S. Lewis, *Mere Christianity*, 1952.

We live in an increasingly permissive society because vast numbers of our people have embraced the belief that there is no God—or, at least, not One Who could hold anyone accountable or punish anyone for any personal activity.

☙❧

"Who died…?"

God died—or so they think. And if God is dead, you can make yourself god—god of as much as you can control—whoever you are. We live in a world where many, many people are making themselves god of as much as they can. They do what they want to do, whatever the consequences. They take what they want, regardless of whom it actually belongs to. They don't do what they should do, because they don't want to, and expect others to make up the difference—which is less and less likely to happen as more and more people make themselves gods. Multiply it a million times, and then imagine what the result will be when everybody makes himself or herself god.

Or don't imagine it—just look around.

Of course, not everybody who has been made god will have to answer "Me," when asked, "Who made you God?" Because God has died—as far as many people are concerned—some people have figured out that they can be god of more than themselves, if they have the money to buy more power, or the celebrity to claim more influence, or the political clout to be elected or appointed to more authority.

If you can get people to make you god over more—over other people—then you will get a real sense of what gods can do. And if, in those high places of power, you do not have to submit to a higher power—a supreme, divine Power—like a *real* God—what you are permitted to do will seem—and perhaps be—unlimited. You can alter the lives of countless millions and undermine the moral foundations of great nations.

And more and more, we see what it looks like for people to act as though they are God.

Those with no real power are pathetic in their immoral posturing; those with great power imperil us all with their hubris.

❧

Job had good reason to wonder if God had died. He called out to his God over and over again and his God did not come. God did not reveal Himself to Job or answer Job in his distress—until the end.

In the end, it became clear that God was not dead. Nor had He "delegated" His divinity—to Job or any other human being who might have wanted to take God's place.

Throughout the Book of Job, Job had been demanding answers from God. When God appears to Job, it is God Who asks the questions.

Today, many have decided, consciously or otherwise, that there is no God, in any practical sense, and any book of revelation claiming to be from this God and about this God can safely be ignored. It's all a bunch of outdated superstitions, legends and mythology, they smugly conclude. And everyone does what is right in his or her own eyes—again.[161]

❧

But suppose that—contrary to popular opinion—God is not dead.

A newspaper once told all its readers that Mark Twain had died. In response, the quite healthy humorist wrote, "The report of my death was an exaggeration."[162] Is the report of God's death not also "an exaggeration"—so exaggerated as to be totally untrue?

---

[161] Judges 21:25.
[162] In Samuel L. Clemons' letter to a *New York Journal* reporter, June 2, 1897.

From Job 40

Billy Graham once said, "I know that God is alive because I spoke with Him this morning."[163]

The Apostle Paul says, *"...what can be known about God is plain to them, because God has shown it to them. For his invisible attributes, namely, his eternal power and divine nature, have been clearly perceived, ever since the creation of the world, in the things that have been made. So they are without excuse. For although they knew God, they did not honor him as God or give thanks to him, but they became futile in their thinking, and their foolish hearts were darkened. Claiming to be wise, they became fools...."*[164]

❦

We have the most educated society the world has ever seen. Our understanding of astronomy, geology, biology and psychology are significantly greater than what was known in biblical times. The taken-for-granted, technical gizmos of our day would have seemed like inexplicable, spectacular magic a hundred years ago—much less, a thousand years ago—or three.

And yet, claiming to be wise, we have become fools—if we claim that God is dead and think that we can put ourselves—or anybody else—in His place.

Twice fools.

First, for thinking God could die—or that He never existed—while everything else, including us, has been caused to exist and continues to be so.

Second, for assuming that, in the absence of an eternal, omnipotent, omniscient God, infinite in love and grace, any one (or combination) of us small, sad mortals could keep the world running without running it off the rails.

"Have you an arm like God? Can you thunder with a voice like His?" God asks Job—and us.

---

[163] In response to a question on *The Today Show* in the 1960s about "the Death of God" controversy, recounted in *Reaching Generation Next: Effective Evangelism in Today's Culture*, Lewis A. Drummond, 2002.
[164] Romans 1:19-22, ESV.

Not hardly.

So why is everybody so determined to do away with God these days?

Perhaps the answer to that question is contained in another question that God puts to Job: *"Will you condemn Me that you may be in the right?"*

❧

If there is a God—a real, true, honest-to-God God—nobody else gets to be God. Period. End of discussion.

And if this real God has put out the final word on right and wrong—and it's "one size fits all"—and you're out of step with God's moral cadence—you've got to "skip to" to get in step—or face God's wrath for marching to the beat of a different drummer.

Claiming to be wise, we become fools.[165]

The Supreme Court can create laws, for instance, but it cannot make them moral, if they violate the moral code of God. The stars of Hollywood can fill our TVs and movie screens with their darkness and debauchery, but one day, they will all answer for their behavior before the God Who filled the universe with real stars.

We trade spiritual faith for secular sophistication and think that the apparent absence of God is evidence that we don't need God because we are able to do God's job ourselves.

God is not absent—though He may be unseen.[166] God is not dead—because He was and is and ever will be.[167] God is not dead, and we are not gods. We are not gods because God is God.[168]

Only He is God and He is the only God[169]—no matter how many people try to make themselves or anyone else God instead. You cannot make anybody else God, no matter how often and how

---

[165] Romans 1:22.
[166] John 1:18.
[167] Revelation 4:8.
[168] Psalm 100:3.
[169] Isaiah 45:18.

From Job 40

low you bow down before that person. And you cannot make yourself God, no matter how often and how flagrantly you ignore and violate God's law.

☙❧

In the end, God appeared to Job.

In the end—if not before—God will appear to every one of us. If you don't like the way God has guided things in your life, you'll have a chance to tell Him so.[170]

But be careful there—a lot of what we think has gone wrong in our lives is *our* fault, not God's. We do more damage to ourselves and others by competing with God for the role of God than He does while guiding our lives within the flow of history and Creation.

And if God allows our suffering here, know that those who acknowledge His Lordship here will receive crowns and thrones in heaven surrounding His throne,[171] not as those who tried to make themselves gods, but as disciples of the God Who became like us and suffered for us so that we might reign in heaven forever with Him.

Who died and made you God?

Nobody.

Who died and made you God's beloved and redeemed child?

Now *that's* a very different question with a very different and wonderful answer: The God Who was dead—on a Cross and in a tomb—and is alive for evermore.[172]

☙❧

---

[170] Matthew 25:31-33; Hebrews 9:27.
[171] James 1:12; 1 Peter 5:4; Revelation 20:4.
[172] Revelation 1:18.

Is That Your Final Answer?

Job 42:1-6 NRSV

> [1] Then Job answered the LORD and said:
> [2] "I know that you can do all things,
>   and that no purpose of yours can be thwarted.
> [3] 'Who is this that hides counsel without knowledge?'
>   Therefore I have uttered what I did not understand,
>   things too wonderful for me, which I did not know.
> [4] 'Hear, and I will speak;
>   I will question you, and you make it known to me.'
> [5] I had heard of you by the hearing of the ear,
>   but now my eye sees you;
> [6] therefore I despise myself,
>   and repent in dust and ashes."

21.

Is That Your Final Answer?

Job 42:1-6 NRSV

Well—we're back to Job this morning. You remember that happy camper "from the merry ol' land of Oz"—or Uz. Job's wonderful world falls apart—is *torn* apart—and it isn't long before everybody wants to give him advice. Everybody's got the answer to Job's problem.

Of course, Job has a few answers for them. Actually, you can boil all of his answers down to one answer: "No!"

Job argues with his increasingly unsympathetic buddies throughout the book with his name on it, rejecting everything they have to say about his predicament until, finally, Job gets what he wants. Job wants a face-to-face showdown with God, and, in the end, he gets it. But it doesn't sound like he likes what he gets.

Job has a few key questions for God, and Job wants some straight answers.

But he isn't going to get them. God has brought some questions of His own to the courtroom, and all of a sudden, Job is the one squirming on the hot seat—dust and ashes and boils and all.

Job wants some answers, but all he is going to get from God is questions and more questions. And these aren't the easy-to-answer kinds of question. God is asking what might as well be rhetorical questions because God knows that Job can't answer them.

Job has been demanding to know why God is doing what He's doing to Job. And if God isn't actually, directly, doing the damage (which Job is certainly not convinced of), why is God at least allowing all the bad stuff to happen to Job?

Seems like a fair question, but God ignores it. God stirs up a tornado and speaks to Job from within it, drowning out the roar of the storm in a Voice that could and did create worlds, just by speaking.[173]

This is not exactly the best venue for a calmly considered exchange of views. No "still, small voice" from God[174] on this day. And God doesn't waste any time taking Job on about the way the world was created and how it's running now.

It's a breathtaking display of divine power and holy imagination, with "foundations of the earth" and "morning stars," "gates of death" and "storehouses of snow." And when God has finished His response to Job's challenge, Job, the lowly man who stands, doggedly, in the presence of this awesome God, clears his throat to answer. Job's voice cannot compete with the raging wind. But for all that, he will be heard. God hears when you speak to Him, whatever else is going on.[175]

Job has said many things to other people about God. He has said many things to an absent God about what he has experienced in the life God has given him. And now Job will offer his final answer to God as God confronts him—face to face.

"I know that you can do all things and that no purpose of yours can be thwarted," Job tells God.

That's fair enough. God will have His way. And God certainly made a convincing case for His power in the word pictures He painted for Job.

---

[173] Genesis 1.
[174] 1 Kings 19:11-12.
[175] Psalm 4:3.

From Job 42

And Job continues, *"I have uttered what I did not understand, things too wonderful for me, which I did not know."* There's no shame in admitting that, either; everybody else is in the same boat. You only know about God what God wants you to know about Him.[176] It's called "revelation."

And along that same line, Job says to God, *"I had heard of you by the hearing of the ear, but now my eye sees you."* All his life, Job had been nurtured in the fear and admonition of the Lord.[177] All his life, he had been told what to believe and how to act in order to satisfy God's requirements of him, so that he would be a good and acceptable child of the sacred covenant with God.

❦

But a lifetime of training and tradition *about* God is nothing compared to a moment of personal encounter *with* God. What do you know about God that you didn't read or hear from someone else? What do you know of God from personal experience? Have you seen God—face to face?[178]

Job had.

And so he answered God by acknowledging God's unequalled majesty—and by confessing his own human inadequacy—and by affirming the spiritual transformation his encounter with God produced.

Now let me say here that the final part of Job's final answer—verse six in our reading today—is to some degree a mystery. The Bible in the pew renders it, *"I despise myself and repent in dust and ashes."* But the original Hebrew is vague and there are almost as many translations as there are translators.

According to the Hebrew scholars, Job certainly despises or abhors or loathes something, but it's not clear what. It could be

---

[176] Deuteronomy 29:29.
[177] Ephesians 6:4.
[178] Exodus 33:11.

himself, his life, his misfortunes, even his earlier arguments and attitudes.

And he either repents of something, or rejects it or retracts it, whether it's his human frailty or his grief or his challenge of God. Job is either offering God his total submission or accepting God's defense of Himself or deciding that it's time to call a halt to his own efforts to prove his innocence. As a final answer, we could wish for more clarity.

And the same is true, really, of God's answer to Job. God comes and offers Job a spectacular summary of His cosmic power and sovereignty. This God is an awesome God.[179] As the Psalmist says, *"How majestic is [his] name in all the earth."*[180]

But, for all that, God does not address Job's concern. God does not answer the question that Job's pain and sorrow and humiliation raise about God's concern for Job as God's faithful servant. As a final answer, God's answer to Job is not very satisfactory.

Fortunately, God's answer to Job turns out *not* to be God's final answer. God's final answer would come years—centuries—after Job, and would start off sounding a lot like Job's question: "Why?" There would come a day, when another servant of God, a blameless and upright Man for Whom the phrase "no one like Him on earth" would be even truer than it was of Job.

God's final answer began in the form of a Man in the midst of losing everything, a *"man of sorrows...acquainted with grief,"*[181] a Man Whose body was wracked with pain, calling out to God much as Job had, *"My God, my God, why have you forsaken me?"*[182]

---

[179] See "Our God is an Awesome God," by Rich Mullins, 1988.
[180] Psalm 8:1, 9, RSV.
[181] Isaiah 53.3, RSV.
[182] Matthew 27:46, from Psalm 22:1, ESV.

From Job 42

God's final answer to Job and to all the Jobs of this world came, not from the whirlwind, but from the Cross. And that final answer to our sorrow and suffering and inability to understand our lot in life was completed in another unexpected encounter between a skeptical man and an awesome God. The episode is recorded in the 20th chapter of the Gospel of John.[183]

Three days after that cry of dereliction on the Cross, God in the Person of Jesus Christ, crucified and resurrected, appeared to His tormented and terrified followers. And this time, God is not showing them the splendors of the universe He created, but the nail scars in His hands. This time, God is not proving His preeminence, He is providing peace and purpose and the power of the Holy Spirit.

Do you suffer?

God's answer is, "I suffered more—for you."

Is your life miserable?

God's answer is, *"I am come that [you] might have life, and…have it more abundantly."*[184]

❧

In the depth of his despair, Job hoped and prayed for a redeemer who would overcome his agony and restore his relationship with God.[185] And that Redeemer did, at last, stand upon the earth. He was God's Final Answer.

But there was one, like Job, who would not be satisfied with what he heard from others. Like Job, he would have to see God face to face.

"Now Thomas, one of the twelve…was not with them when Jesus came." Later, Thomas *"said to them, 'Unless I see in his hands the print of the nails…and place my hand in his side, I will not believe.'"*[186]

---

[183] John 20:19-31.
[184] John 10:10, KJV.
[185] Job 19:25.
[186] John 20:24-25, RSV.

You know the story: A week after the Resurrection, Jesus again appeared to the disciples and Thomas was there this time. Jesus told Thomas, *"Put your finger here, and see my hands; and reach out your hand, and place it in my side. Do not doubt, but believe."*[187]

And if there is any uncertainty about Job's final answer, there is none about the answer Thomas gave. He responded to God's Final Answer with his own: *"My Lord and my God!"*[188]

It's the right answer, finally, and is probably what Job was trying to say in that ancient and uncertain text. Job and Thomas both saw the glory of God and believed because of what they saw. Job believed God would take care of him—and Thomas believed that God already had.

※

And what about you?

In the midst of your pain or hardship, your disappointment and sorrow, it's pretty normal to wonder what God is up to. Sometimes, the second-hand reports just don't get the job done; you have to go looking for God yourself and refuse to give up until you see Him face-to-face. What other people say doesn't really matter, in the end. It's what God says to you that matters.

Now you know God's Final Answer: *"…Jesus Christ and Him Crucified…"*[189]—for you.

What will your final answer be to Him?

※

---

[187] John 20:27, RSV.
[188] John 20:28, RSV.
[189] 1 Corinthians 2:2.

From the Book of Proverbs

Proverbs 3:5-8 ESV

The Book of Proverbs contains a vast collection of practical and proven insights about how to live successfully. Today's reading provides a summary of the life that is lived according to this system.

> *⁵ Trust in the* LORD *with all your heart,*
>   *and do not lean on your own understanding.*
> *⁶ In all your ways acknowledge him,*
>   *and he will make straight your paths.*
> *⁷ Be not wise in your own eyes;*
>   *fear the* LORD, *and turn away from evil.*
> *⁸ It will be healing to your flesh*
>   *and refreshment to your bones.*

Matthew 7:24-27 ESV

Jesus concludes the Sermon on the Mount with a dire warning about the dangers of rejecting the wisdom of God as the foundation for a secure and successful life.

[Jesus said:]

²⁴ "Everyone then who hears these words of mine and does them will be like a wise man who built his house on the rock. ²⁵ And the rain fell, and the floods came, and the winds blew and beat on that house, but it did not fall, because it had been founded on the rock. ²⁶ And everyone who hears these words of mine and does not do them will be like a foolish man who built his house on the sand. ²⁷ And the rain fell, and the floods came, and the winds blew and beat against that house, and it fell, and great was the fall of it."

22.

The Wisest Thing You'll Ever Do

Proverbs 3:5-8; Matthew 7:24-27 ESV

Andy Griffith died this week. As the newspaper said, his was a brilliant career, and the pinnacle of that career was spent in a fictional town called Mayberry, with a population of very funny—and very fine—people, living together in a way that turned out, time and again, to be unexpectedly wise, in spite of their individual foibles.

Week after week, for those who watched, there were lessons in living, taught with a humorous touch in the school of human nature, and occasionally explained for clarity by Andy to his on-screen son, Opie. We thought we were being entertained; what it was, was "character education."[190]

I found myself this week trying to imagine Sheriff Andy Taylor reading the Book of Proverbs to Opie in that familiar North Carolina twang. It would have to have been an updated translation, of course, and heavy on the homespun phrases that were his stock in trade. But it would not have been out of character, because much of Proverbs is presented as a heart-to-heart talk between a devoted father and the son he loves.

---

[190] An appreciative take-off on Andy Griffith's early comedic monologue, "What It Was, Was Football," 1953.

Proverbs is a talk that every father should have with every son, and—with the appropriate adjustments—every mother with every daughter. Many of the problems in the homes and schools and communities across our country are the result of parents not having this conversation with their young children—not having it early enough, and not having it often enough. The conversation is about wisdom, something children don't have, but desperately need. And the sooner they get it, the better.

Children need wisdom—actually, we all do—because there is a danger out there (in the world)—and in here (in our hearts)—that will destroy anyone who doesn't have the kind of wisdom Proverbs talks about. The danger is temptation—the very real, seductive appeal that comes from within and is augmented by all sorts of tempters around us to do the things we want so much to do, but that wreck our lives if we do them.

And what is the father in the Bible so concerned to warn his son about—time and time again?

Oh, just those outdated things like peer pressure, materialism, and casual sex.

Don't over-spiritualize the book and message of Proverbs. The parent in Proverbs is trying to prevent his child from ruining his life—because every child approaching adulthood is at risk of doing just that—because the desire for sinful, destructive things is alive in every human heart, and the world is full of evil people, young and old, who will line up for the chance to draw others into lives of the lowest conduct and sickest perspectives.

The Proverbs parent is still fighting for the heart of his child—the soul of his child—the most honorable and highest possibility of his child's life. That parent is pointing out all the dangers—again and again and again—and pointing out all the people who will gladly entice that child to choose the way of destruction.

From Proverbs 3

Today, parents don't seem to have the wisdom to realize that their children must be constantly confronted with the need to seek wisdom, to desire wisdom, to embrace wisdom. Or they don't have the courage to take on all the voices seducing their children to self-destructive behavior. Or they don't know what to say to compete with the world's winsome appeal, or how to stand up to their children's natural human willfulness.

And so we allow friendships that will certainly sow the seeds of bad character. We feed the desire for "things" in the hope this will buy us acceptance and avoid conflict. We fall back on contraception for our children because we have bought the world's lies that sexual urges can't be controlled, and children shouldn't be controlled by responsible parents exactly when the children are least able to exercise self-control themselves.

About the time we started watching Andy raising Opie, the great cultural influencers of our land decided that parents weren't the ones to be raising their own children. The "experts" decided to appoint themselves to take over that job. These experts were actually just overly confident social experimenters. And before long, with their blessing, children were raising themselves, for the most part—at least as far as morality and character, values and attitudes were concerned.

And because these children were allowed to "raise" themselves, they grew up absolutely convinced they were wiser than anybody else.

In the absence of any serious options, a generation of kids grew up…

"trusting *themselves* with all their hearts
and leaning on their own understanding;
in all their ways they acknowledged *themselves*,
assuming *they* could make their own life paths straight."

We have grown a culture that is wise in its own eyes;[191] neither fearing God nor shunning evil.[192] It is the way of the fool. It is the way of destruction, for individuals and societies.

☙❧

But there is another way.

It is the way of wisdom—God's wisdom. And God would have His Church reintroduce it into this pathetic, fool-filled world. Our Heavenly Father would like to have a heart-to-heart talk with His children about their wayward behavior and the attitudes behind it.

We don't have time to hear the whole talk today, but we can summarize.

Wisdom is essential for a successful life. Wisdom is available to all. But wisdom is more than knowing things—even the right things. Part of wisdom is *knowing* the difference between right and wrong (because God has revealed what is right and what is wrong). But wisdom is also *wanting* to do the right so strongly that the urge to live wisely—the way God says to—overwhelms the other urges—the evil desires we all harbor inside that will damage or destroy us if we give into them.

And really, wisdom is even more than knowing what is right and wanting to do right more than you want to do wrong. Proverbs says, *"Trust in the Lord with all your heart,"* and then, *"fear the Lord."* Earlier it says, *"The fear of the Lord is the beginning of wisdom."*[193] Wisdom begins in the right attitude about God. It is "knowing" and "wanting"—and "letting."

Since wisdom belongs to God, it is God Who flips the switch in us (at our request) and turns on our ability to want so much to be obedient in the wise things of God that temptation can be overcome, and tempters can be rejected—if you let Him—if you trust Him.

---

[191] Proverbs 26:12.
[192] See Job 1:1, KJV.
[193] Proverbs 1:7, KJV.

From Proverbs 3

All of life ultimately breaks down to the wise and the foolish. Wisdom begins by trusting in the Lord with all your heart. Wisdom is not what you know—nor what you think. It is not intellect—superior or otherwise.

Wisdom begins in the heart, with convictions, and feelings about those convictions, that motivate acts of trust, and then obedience. Wisdom requires trusting God with all your heart, which means there is no allowable area of *not* trusting. The wisest thing you can do is trust God completely—whatever you think.

And just as you trust God completely, you completely give over the idea that you can figure out this world—this life—*your* life—on your own. Do not lean on your own insight. Do not prop yourself up with any foolish confidence that you can figure out for yourself what is good and right. No matter how clever you are—or *think* you are—something—life, other people, God—something will come along and knock that prop out from under you and down you will go. In all your heart, trust in the Lord; in all your ways, acknowledge Him. "Do" the trust you have embraced with all your heart. Act on it, in everything.

☙❧

It's kind of like piloting an airplane. You contact the control tower for clearance to take off every time you want to fly, because the tower has the best vantage point to know if it is safe for you to do so.

And throughout the course of your flight you stay in contact with the air traffic controller because the controller knows where you are in relation to all the hazards of the flight and your progress toward your goal.

We do not make our paths straight. God does. Only God knows what straight is.

Someone I know is fond of saying that "God writes straight with crooked lines." It is a Portuguese proverb that recognizes that God applies a divine wisdom to overcome the messes we make

The Wisest Thing You'll Ever Do

when we act in our own wisdom. But to the degree that we trust God and accept His teaching about wisdom, and live in His wisdom, our crooked lines will be straighter to begin with.

The Father tells His child, *"Do not be wise in your own eyes."* But how hard that is to obey! There is no one more sure of his own wisdom than the fool—from Solomon to the present day—no one more susceptible to the lies of a tempter than one who has decided already to believe that the lies are true.

And like Eve in the Garden,[194] we all see things that we desire, thinking they will make us wise. And, oh, how we want to be wise without God's help and contrary to His spoken will!

The wisest thing you'll ever do is reject the idea that there is any wisdom other than God's wisdom. The wisest thing you'll ever do is trust in God's wisdom and reject your own. The wisest thing you'll ever do is want the wisdom of God more than your own desires.

Not the easiest thing, but the wisest.

---

[194] Genesis 3:1-6.

Proverbs 15:1-5 ESV

> *¹ A soft answer turns away wrath,*
>   *but a harsh word stirs up anger.*
> *² The tongue of the wise commends knowledge,*
>   *but the mouths of fools pour out folly.*
> *³ The eyes of the* LORD *are in every place,*
>   *keeping watch on the evil and the good.*
> *⁴ A gentle tongue is a tree of life,*
>   *but perverseness in it breaks the spirit.*
> *⁵ A fool despises his father's instruction,*
>   *but whoever heeds reproof is prudent.*

A Word To (and From) the Wise

James 3:6-18 ESV

⁶ *And the tongue is a fire, a world of unrighteousness. The tongue is set among our members, staining the whole body, setting on fire the entire course of life, and set on fire by hell.* ⁷ *For every kind of beast and bird, of reptile and sea creature, can be tamed and has been tamed by mankind,* ⁸ *but no human being can tame the tongue. It is a restless evil, full of deadly poison.* ⁹ *With it we bless our Lord and Father, and with it we curse people who are made in the likeness of God.* ¹⁰ *From the same mouth come blessing and cursing. My brothers, these things ought not to be so.* ¹¹ *Does a spring pour forth from the same opening both fresh and salt water?* ¹² *Can a fig tree, my brothers, bear olives, or a grapevine produce figs? Neither can a salt pond yield fresh water.*

¹³ *Who is wise and understanding among you? By his good conduct let him show his works in the meekness of wisdom.* ¹⁴ *But if you have bitter jealousy and selfish ambition in your hearts, do not boast and be false to the truth.* ¹⁵ *This is not the wisdom that comes down from above, but is earthly, unspiritual, demonic.* ¹⁶ *For where jealousy and selfish ambition exist, there will be disorder and every vile practice.* ¹⁷ *But the wisdom from above is first pure, then peaceable, gentle, open to reason, full of mercy and good fruits, impartial and sincere.* ¹⁸ *And a harvest of righteousness is sown in peace by those who make peace.*

23.

A Word To (and From) the Wise

Proverbs 15:1-5; James 3:6-18 ESV

The Bible is the Word of God, inspired and inspiring. It begins with the majestic creation of the World[195] and ends with the glorious consummation of History.[196] In between, it tells the story of God's chosen people and the providential coming of the Christ,[197] the Word made flesh to dwell among us[198] and deliver us who believe in Him from eternal damnation.[199] The Bible is full of mighty miracles and powerful prophecies and the life-giving gospel of Jesus…

…and advice about how to talk nice.

Somewhere near the middle of the Bible—right after all the great and soaring psalms—there is a collection of simple sayings, practical wisdom broken down into bite-sized morsels: the Book of Proverbs. Put together by the sharpest minds in the kingdom, its purpose is to give young people a leg up on practical success in

---

[195] Genesis 1.
[196] Revelation 21:1.
[197] Luke 2:8:11.
[198] John 1:14.
[199] John 3:16.

A Word To (and From) the Wise

life. Chapter after chapter, parental advice pours forth: "Do this!" "Don't do that!" "Be wise, my son. Listen to what I'm telling you."

There are 31 chapters of these proverbs in the Book of Proverbs—one for every day of the longest months—which would make it easy for a father to read to his son a chapter every day—or have the son read it for himself when he's old enough—and repeat the process every month as the child grows up.

Much of the material actually repeats itself, chapter after chapter, as though the wise men who put the proverbs together didn't think much of the typical attention span of young people. (And this was before smart phones, social media and video games.) Or maybe, they just thought the main things were so important for the future that they should focus the kids of the kingdom more on the key concepts than anything else.

And so, somewhere near the middle of the book—at the beginning of Chapter 15—you find the wisdom you heard today: *"A soft answer turns away wrath, but a harsh word stirs up anger."*

❧

This is not the first time the idea turns up in Proverbs and it won't be the last, but it does turn up here, and it is an awful lot of wisdom in very few words. And if we, whatever our ages, hear it and heed it, we're likely to get a little—or a lot—wiser, even now, and a whole lot more successful in life, however much more of our lives we still have before us. Part of the wisdom of the Proverbs is the recognition that, though they are presented to the young, they remain profoundly wise for people of all ages.

And a couple of other things: You don't put a proverb in the Bible about the right way to do something if everybody is already doing it the right way all the time anyway. In other words, "if it ain't broke, the Bible doesn't try get you to fix it."

And, secondly, if something *is* broke, but it *can't* be fixed, there's no point telling people they *ought* to fix it—or how they should do so.

From Proverbs 15

So, if the Bible says what it says about soft answers and hard words, it must mean that most people have problems in this area, and that we really can do something productive about it. And that being the case, let's spend our Sunday morning looking into this "word of wisdom" from the wise men of the Bible and see if we can learn how to make our words wiser as well.

❦

The first part of the Proverb says, "*A soft answer turns away wrath...*" Six words—fewer in the original Hebrew. One of these words is "answer." The proverb begins not with you starting a conversation, but with your response to something said by someone else. And maybe it isn't the first answer in the interchange. Most of the time, most people are involved in an exchange that is well underway. For that reason, answers are important—even crucial.

But unlike the first thing said, answers always come in the context of what has already been said—and how it was said—and heard. And answers determine what will happen next.

Communication experts will tell you what you already know: Conversations have informational content—and emotional content. There is *what* we say and there is *how* we say it—conveying (in tone, volume, vocabulary or other means) how we feel about what we say—or sometimes even, how we feel that has nothing to do with what we say.

The conversation implied in the proverb is one in which the other person is upset: He or she has "wrath." Most people don't like dealing with people who are mad—especially if they're mad at you—or pointing their anger *at* you.

What do you do? How do you answer wrath?

Our human inclination is the "poker approach": "I'll 'see' your 'wrath' and 'raise' you two more!" We are inclined to respond in kind, and even escalate things a bit, just to show how much we don't appreciate being on the receiving end of somebody else's anger. We tend to think that giving someone some of his own medicine is the best way to turn an undesirable attitude off.

It isn't, of course; it usually just makes matters worse. The wise word is "soft." *"A soft answer turns away wrath."*

So what is a "soft" answer?

Certainly not a weak one. It's not "caving in." But "soft" *is* the opposite of "hard"—or "abrasive." "Soft" suggests "gentle," "pleasant," "comforting." I've even seen some "paper products" advertised as "soft and absorbent."

A soft answer is a response to anger that absorbs the negative energy rather than intensifying it. The soft answer—the wise answer—waits till the sting of the other person's wrathful words subside before deciding what would be best to say back.

A soft answer can diffuse an already bad situation. It turns away wrath because it refuses to send anger back all fueled up for another lap around "the emotional track." To make your answer "soft" when you feel your own wrathful response welling up within you requires far more strength than forming the more instinctive "hard" answer. But if your goal is to turn away wrath—as it should be—the soft answer is the wise answer.

It's like Rudyard Kipling wrote his son:
> "If you can keep your head when all about you
> are losing theirs and blaming it on you...."[200]

(*If—*)

Your answers can be soft—and therefore wise—when you keep your head. *"A soft answer turns away wrath."*

❧

"But a harsh word stirs up anger."

This time, seven words—but, again, less in Hebrew. And as is typical with Hebrew poetry, the rhyme is in the ideas, not the sound of the last words in the lines.

---

[200] Rudyard Kipling, "If-," 1895.

From Proverbs 15

But this second line of the proverb is not a carbon copy in meaning to the first line. If anything, it's the flipside. From an "answer" to a "word." From "soft" to "harsh" (the Hebrew word also means "painful"). From turning away and diffusing negative emotions to stirring them up.

In this phrase, the word, "word," is singular. One word can do the trick. One word is enough to stir up anger, if it's harsh or causes pain. Whoever said, "Sticks and stones can break my bones, but words can never hurt me," never got hit with the right words. The right word—or wrong word, as the case may be—can "do you in." One harsh word.

The most dangerous word to speak may be the first word, if it is the beginning of words filled with anger, hostility, disrespect or ridicule. So many words are best left unspoken. Harsh or hurtful words rarely help anything. They rarely make the person who speaks them feel better for long, because what comes next rarely resolves the hurt or anger that motivated the wrong words to start with. Harsh words, as we said a moment ago, do not invite soft answers in reply.

Maybe that's why my mother always told me, "You can catch more flies with honey than you can with vinegar." And even though I never understood why anybody would want to catch more flies, I did get the point that my words should be sweet and not sour or bitter.

Another thing to realize is that the anger a harsh word may stir up may not be related to *that* particular harsh word at all. Many of us have unresolved emotions from past experiences—other conversations—recent or long past—that we try to store someplace out of the way, so we can get on with our lives. If we can keep the conversation pleasant—civil—all will be well.

But a harsh word can be like the match that sets a forest ablaze. You didn't dry out the pine straw, but your little flame still started something terrible you didn't expect—and may not be able to resolve.

But who decides when a word is harsh?

Unfortunately, the person who hears it decides, not the one who speaks it. You may not think that fair, but that's the way it works. If you're the one who hears someone else, and you experience what is said as harsh, you will not wait for that person or a third party to tell you whether it was or not.

Nor will anyone wait for "the referee" when you say something that seems to him or her to be offensive. As you prepare to speak, remember that the listener always "calls the fouls," never the speaker.

⁂

And yet, we must speak. We speak to live. We speak to accomplish those things that require the help of others. We speak to serve our Lord.

It has been said that "our eyes are the windows into our soul."[201] If that is so, our tongues—to hear James tell it in his epistle—are often the plumbing coming out of it. James had nothing good to say about the tongue because it causes all of us so much trouble—as individuals, families and church fellowships.

For that reason, we must be wise enough to know that we must give more attention—more effort—more consideration—more self-discipline to what we express and how we express it. Freedom of speech is something we rightly demand from our government, but we should never allow ourselves unfettered freedom to say whatever we feel compelled to say at any moment.

Each of us should carefully supervise ourselves in all we are inclined to say to ensure that no harsh word slips out that did not need to be spoken—or written. We should consider each answer to what has been said to us, so that we turn away wrath rather than venting our own.

---

[201] The proverb has been attributed to the Roman orator Cicero, Jesus, Leonardo Da Vinci and William Shakespeare, among others.

"But they're wrong and I'm right!"
So?
"But I care very deeply about what I'm saying!"
So?
"But it's just so hard to control what I say."
So?
"But you don't know what they said to me?"

No, but I know that God does, because God is present to hear every word spoken in every conversation, everywhere in the world. *"The eyes of the Lord are in every place"*—and His ears, too. And I know that God, Who has heard it all, says,

>*"A soft answer turns away wrath,*
>*but a harsh word stirs up anger."*

It's the wise word for you and for me and for our church. Honest! From God's mouth to your ear!

From the Book of Ecclesiastes

Ecclesiastes 1:1-14 ESV

¹ *The words of the Preacher, the son of David, king in Jerusalem.*
² *Vanity of vanities, says the Preacher,*
  vanity of vanities! All is vanity.
³ *What does man gain by all the toil*
  at which he toils under the sun?
⁴ *A generation goes, and a generation comes,*
  but the earth remains forever.
⁵ *The sun rises, and the sun goes down,*
  and hastens to the place where it rises.
⁶ *The wind blows to the south*
  and goes around to the north;
around and around goes the wind,
  and on its circuits the wind returns.
⁷ *All streams run to the sea,*
  but the sea is not full;
to the place where the streams flow,
  there they flow again.
⁸ *All things are full of weariness;*
  a man cannot utter it;
the eye is not satisfied with seeing,
  nor the ear filled with hearing.
⁹ *What has been is what will be,*
  and what has been done is what will be done,
  and there is nothing new under the sun.
¹⁰ *Is there a thing of which it is said,*
  "See, this is new"?
It has been already
  in the ages before us.

Is That All There Is?

> ^{11} There is no remembrance of former things,
> nor will there be any remembrance
> of later things yet to be
> among those who come after.

^{12} I the Preacher have been king over Israel in Jerusalem. ^{13} And I applied my heart to seek and to search out by wisdom all that is done under heaven. It is an unhappy business that God has given to the children of man to be busy with. ^{14} I have seen everything that is done under the sun, and behold, all is vanity and a striving after wind.

24.

Is That All There Is?

Ecclesiastes 1:1-14 ESV

The Book of Ecclesiastes is the most bizarre book in the Bible. It ignores all the history of God's dealings with Israel. It ignores the Law God gave to Moses. It ignores the message of the prophets. It talks about wisdom—using your reason to figure life out—but then it denies that human reason is of any value for that sort of figuring, no matter how wise you are.

And God?

If there is One, He is far away, physically and emotionally, and He's not going to reveal Himself to you.

The author of Ecclesiastes, a Jewish philosopher known as Qoheleth, which means "the Teacher" or "Schoolmaster"—rejects faith, hope—even heaven. There's nothing there, he says. Life—everything—is meaningless. It's a weird book to be in the Bible.

So how did it get there?

※

Well, Qoheleth takes on the persona of King Solomon in the first few chapters, and that connection with Solomon was probably enough to get the book included in the Hebrew canon. The author presents himself as Solomon because, as Solomon—who was, of

Is That All There Is?

course, the wealthiest, most politically powerful, personally pampered and intellectually adept person who ever lived (in Israel's experience, at least)—Qoheleth can play the jaded cynic and present himself as someone who could *have*—or *try*—everything people think will bring meaning to life—and then dismiss it all as totally useless.

Books associated with Solomon did well when they were putting the Bible together. In addition, the last paragraph of the book turns everything around and tells people to fear God and keep His commandments, no matter what the rest of the book says. So Ecclesiastes made it in.

But *how* Ecclesiastes got in the Bible is less important than *why*. If you believe, as I do, that every word in the Bible is the inspired Word of God, the divine answer is more important than the human one. Ecclesiastes is in the Bible because God wanted it there—and wants it there still. It is part of His revelation to us, even though Qoheleth doesn't think God "does" revelation. There is something there in the Book of Ecclesiastes, *from* God, *for* us.

❦

The Book of Ecclesiastes is the most bizarre—but its message is the most modern.

Reading Ecclesiastes is like reading the editorial page of your newspaper or listening to many of the faculty members in colleges across the country—including those in a lot of religion departments: "Life is meaningless!"

To hear the intelligentsia tell it, "There's no point to anything most people have always thought was important in life. Hard work isn't worth the effort. Trying to make something of yourself is a fool's errand. Religion is a waste of time."

And if you start to argue, they say: "No. Don't even start. I know better than you do. I've 'been there and done that.' I've found nothing of value in life, and I'm an expert. Trust me: Life is meaningless. Everything is meaningless."

From Ecclesiastes 1

"Everything is meaningless." That's the latest in post-modern, smug and superior sophistication. It's a mindset that is sweeping the secular scene like a California wildfire[202]—but with far graver consequences. And what the elites in society embrace, the rank and file accept without question, grateful that someone has clued them in to the latest and greatest in worldly wisdom, no matter what it really means for them.

For the modern Qoheleth, there is no Creation; there is merely the cold, mechanical Cosmos.[203] Human beings do not bear the image of God; they are just another species of animal.

There is no divine revelation—or divine Revealer, for that matter; just the accelerating discovery of data through the systematic application of empirical science.

But is this current conviction about the meaninglessness of life the latest and final truth?

Not by a few thousand years. Qoheleth was singing the same old song long before the birth of Jesus, singing with all the certainty of one who knows for sure when he really doesn't know at all.

This teacher was telling his students that everything is meaningless because rivers run to the sea, but never fill it up. What he didn't know about was this business of evaporation and condensation, and that the point of rivers flowing with water is not to fill up the oceans, but to keep the earth and everything on it watered and alive. That's what flowing rivers mean.

Qoheleth knew everything was meaningless because the wind blows in all directions.

What he didn't understand was barometric pressure and weather fronts and the way this special planet maintains an atmosphere that sustains life. That's what the wind means.

---

[202] Several major wildfires were "sweeping" across California the week this sermon was preached.
[203] See the Carl Sagan documentary, *Cosmos: A Personal Voyage*, 1980.

This great sage sounds like somebody out of *Fiddler on the Roof*: "Sunrise…Sunset…"[204]

"The sun just does the same thing day after day—and has—and will—forever. And there's nothing new under the sun, so there's nothing meaningful under it, either."

What he didn't know was that it is the earth that is always on the move around the sun, and that this breathtakingly mathematically precise orbit of ours makes possible the light and heat and gravity that makes possible all life on earth—which is, as far as we know, all the life in the universe.

"But we know all that now," say the modern Qoheleths, "and infinitely more."

⋙⋘

…which is not really true, because "infinite knowledge" is, and will always be, beyond all of us, because we are finite beings with finite minds. For all we know, we will never know all there is to know. And because there will always be that which we do not know, we will never know for sure what—or exactly how much—we do not know.

And here's where *all* the Qoheleths—whether of the biblical or the modern variety—make their crucial mistake: Even if everything you know tells you everything about this world and your life in it is meaningless, you don't know that what you don't know wouldn't prove the exact opposite to be true. It may be that something you *don't* know would prove that life in general and your life in particular is actually incredibly meaningful.

I don't play poker, but I understand that the outcome of the game is determined not merely by the cards you can see, but by the ones you can't see as well. Don't make the mistake of thinking that the cards you can see in life are the only cards in play.

---

[204] Jerry Bock and Sheldon Harnick, *Fiddler on the Roof*, 1964.

From Ecclesiastes 1

If you believe life has no meaning or purpose, you live your life that way. And when you live that way, the life that might have had meaning—was probably intended—created—to have meaning—is wasted.

And if you decide that *your* life has no meaning, will you not also likely decide that the lives of other people have *less* than no meaning—and treat *them* accordingly?

We saw again this week, in Colorado,[205] where that perspective can lead.

And yet, Qoheleth persists: "What do you get for all that you do in life?"

A modern cynic would say,

"Another day older and deeper in debt."[206]

But Qoheleth has another frustration in mind: "You live, you die and nobody remembers."

Yes, you live and you die—assuming Jesus tarries—and sooner or later, everyone who ever knew you or remembered you will die as well. No one in the world will remember that you ever lived. But does that mean your life is meaningless—that it will not have mattered?

Qoheleth asked the wrong question. The key question about life is not "*What* does it matter?" but "*Where* does it matter?"

One day—as all of us, cynics and Christians alike, believe—this world, and all of us, will be gone. This whole world will be no more. And so, there is no such thing as "forever" *here*.

But that doesn't mean that this world and the lives we live here will not have mattered. It just means that *where* we and our lives matter, ultimately and forever, is not *here*.

☙❧

---

[205] On July 20, 2012, 12 people were killed and 70 injured in an Aurora, Colorado, movie theater by a single gunman.
[206] A line from the song, "Sixteen Tons," by Merle Travis, 1946.

Is That All There Is?

"I have seen all the things that are done under the sun," pontificates Qoheleth and his contemporary clones, "all of them are meaningless."

To which we may rightly respond with a little skepticism of our own: Are you sure you have seen *all* the things that are done under the sun? Have you really seen them *all*? Have you seen the Creation of this world from nothing by the spoken word of God,[207] and the forming of humanity in God's image,[208] animated by His divine breath?[209] Have you seen God promise, and then cause, a couple old enough to have great-grandchildren to have a child together?[210] Have you seen this same God deliver a people from bondage and death through a sea He parted in two?[211] Have you seen a murderer named Moses mediate a law code to a new nation chosen by God?[212] Have you seen God appoint a shepherd boy to be a king[213] and send prophets to confront kings in the Name of this God[214] Who refused to be portrayed but demanded to be obeyed? Have you seen the writing and collecting of the sacred scriptures of a people made sacred by God, the God Who even made a way for your cynical words to be included among them?

Or have you merely and conveniently seen only what you wanted to see to support the pessimistic perspective you're peddling?

Qoheleths past and present have this tendency to limit the data they will consider to whatever will support their desired result. "Nothing supernatural, please, it might contaminate my observations. Faith is subjective. I only deal in objective facts."

---

[207] Genesis 1:3-26.
[208] Genesis 1:27.
[209] Genesis 2:7.
[210] Genesis 15:4; 17:15-19; 18:9-14; 21:1-3.
[211] Exodus 14.
[212] Exodus 19—20.
[213] 1 Samuel 16:1-13.
[214] 1 Kings 21.

From Ecclesiastes 1

So you have *not* seen all the things that are done under the sun; just the ones you consider proper and acceptable—things that strike you as "objective." In other words, you only play the cards you can see or are willing to look at.

Whatever the shortcomings of the original Qoheleth's analysis, we cannot fault him for missing one critical piece of information that was not available to him, but that has been there, front and center, for all his modern-day disciples. Even if nothing in *his* experience could be called "a new thing," years after Qoheleth's death, a Carpenter would be crucified outside the walls of Jerusalem[215] and then His Body carried to a borrowed tomb,[216] and then days later that Body would be raised by God from the dead to life again,[217] a "thing" done under the sun of Easter morning that hundreds of the Carpenter's disciples eventually saw—and millions of His disciples continue to believe—making it just impossible for them to accept that everything is meaningless, no matter which and how many smug cynics assure them of that fact.

The cynic says, "There is *nothing* new under the sun, and God is too distant, too mysterious, and frankly, too indifferent to reveal anything about Himself or the meaning of our world or our lives."

And yet God says, "Behold, I make all things new. I will dwell with men. I will be close enough to wipe away their tears and give them living water when they thirst"[218]

So, who you gonna go with?

Qoheleth and his crew of secular cynics…

…or the God Who makes all things—including you—new?

---

[215] John 19.
[216] Matthew 27:57-60.
[217] John 20:1-16.
[218] Revelation 21:1-6.

Indices

Sermon Titles in Alphabetical Order

Title	Page

A Fool by Any Other Name 59
A Word To (and From) the Wise 203

Blinded by Strength 21

David's House 77

For Such a Time as This 169

God's Food in the Desert 141

Holy Housecleaning 159
Hope in the Darkness 93

If He Calls You 39
In the House of the Lord 131
Inauguration Day 47
Is That All There Is? 215
Is That Your Final Answer? 187

Lesser Gods—Easier Ways 5
Let a Mother Pray 31
Love is Not Enough 103

Prove It! 13

Sing to God 111

The Forever House 85
The Wisest Thing You'll Ever Do 195
They Could Not Keep Him Out 67
Things That Kings Can't Do 151

What Shall God Give You? 121
Who Died and Made You God? 179

Sermon Texts in Biblical Order

Text	Title	Page

Judges
2:7, 10-14	Lesser Gods—Easier Ways	4
6:11-17	Prove It!	12
13:1-5	Blinded by Strength	19
16:16-30	Blinded by Strength	19

1 Samuel
1:1-20	Let a Mother Pray	29
3:1-10	If He Calls You	37
3:19-21	Let a Mother Pray	30
16:11-13	Inauguration Day	45
25:1-44	A Fool by Any Other Name	55

2 Samuel
5:1-3, 6-7	They Could Not Keep Him Out	66
7:1-16	David's House	74
7:1-16	The Forever House	83
15:13-30	Hope in the Darkness	90
18:24-33	Love is Not Enough	101
23:1-2	Sing to God	111

1 Kings
2:10-12	What Shall God Give You?	120
3:3-14	What Shall God Give You?	120
6:1-38 (*passim*)	In the House of the Lord	128
8:6-11	In the House of the Lord	129
19:1-8	God's Food in the Desert	139

2 Kings
5:1-15	Things That Kings Can't Do	149
22:1-20	Holy Housecleaning	156
23:1-3	Holy Housecleaning	157

Sermon Texts in Biblical Order

Text	Title	Page
Esther		
4:6-16	For Such a Time as This	167
Job		
40:1-14	Who Died and Made You God?	177
42:1-6	Is That Your Final Answer?	186
Proverbs		
3:5-8	The Wisest Thing You'll Ever Do	194
15:1-5	A Word To (and From) the Wise	201
Ecclesiastes		
1:1-14	Is That All There Is?	213

Sermon Texts in Biblical Order

Text	Title	Page
Matthew		
3 1-3, 13-17	Inauguration Day	46
4:1-11	God's Food in the Desert	140
7:13-19	Lesser Gods—Easier Ways	4
7:24-27	The Forever House	84
7:24-27	The Wisest Thing You'll Ever Do	194
Mark		
14:32-36	Hope in the Darkness	92
Luke		
2:41-52	If He Calls You	38
12:13-21	A Fool By Any Other Name	58
15:11-24	Love is Not Enough	102
John		
2:13-22	Holy Housecleaning	158
6:25-30	Prove It!	12
12:12-16	They Could Not Keep Him Out	66
18:28-37	For Such a Time as This	168
Acts		
13:22-23, 32-38	David's House	76
1 Corinthians		
3:9-17	In the House of the Lord	130
Colossians		
3:12-17	Sing to God	112
James		
3:6-18	A Word To (and From) the Wise	202
Revelation		
4:2-11	Who Died and Made You God?	178

Sermon Texts in Lectionary Order

Date	Text	Page
Cycle A		
Advent 2	Matthew 3 1-3, 13-17	46
Baptism of the Lord	Matthew 3 1-3, 13-17	46
Epiphany 7 [7]	1 Corinthians 3:9-17	130
Epiphany 9 [9]	Matthew 7:24-27	84, 194
Lent 1	Matthew 4:1-11	140
Lent 4	1 Samuel 16:11-13	45
Proper 4 [9]	Matthew 7:24-27	84, 194
Proper 12 [17]	1 Kings 3:3-14	120

Sermon Texts in Lectionary Order

Date	Text	Page
Cycle B		
Advent 4	2 Samuel 7:1-16	74, 83
Epiphany 2 [2]	1 Samuel 3:1-10	37
Epiphany 6 [6]	2 Kings 5:1-15	149
Lent 3	John 2:13-22	158
Palm/Passion Sunday	Mark 14:32-36	92
	John 12:12-16	66
Proper 4 [9]	1 Samuel 3:1-10	37
Proper 9 [14]	2 Samuel 5:1-3, 6-7	66
Proper 11 [16]	2 Samuel 7:1-16	74, 83
Proper 14 [19]	2 Samuel 18:24-33	101
	1 Kings 19:1-8	139
Proper 15 [20]	1 Kings 2:10-12; 3:3-14	120
Proper 16 [21]	1 Kings 8:6-11	129
Proper 19 [24]	James 3:6-18	202
Proper 20 [25]	James 3:6-18	202
Proper 25 [30]	Job 42:1-6	186
Proper 28 [33]	1 Samuel 1:1-20	29
Reign of Christ [34]	2 Samuel 23:1-2	111
	John 18:28-37	168

Sermon Texts in Lectionary Order

Date	Text	Page

Cycle C

Christmas 1	Colossians 3:12-17	112
	Luke 2:41-52	38
Lent 4	Luke 15:11-24	102
Proper 7 [12]	1 Kings 19:1-8	139
Proper 9 [14]	2 Kings 5:1-15	149
Proper 13 [18]	Ecclesiastes 1:1-14	213
	Luke 12:13-21	58
Proper 23 [28]	2 Kings 5:1-15	149

Additional Scripture Passages Referenced

Text	Title	Page
Genesis		
1	Is That Your Final Answer?	188
1	A Word To (and From) the Wise	203
1:3-26	Is That All There Is?	220
1:27	Is That All There Is?	220
2:7	Is That All There Is?	220
3:1-6	The Wisest Thing You'll Ever Do	200
6:12-21	If He Calls You	43
11:1-9	*Preface*	ix
15:4	Is That All There Is?	220
17:15-19	Is That All There Is?	220
18:9-14	Is That All There Is?	220
21:1-3	Is That All There Is?	220
28:10-17	If He Calls You	41
Exodus		
3:1-10	If He Calls You	43
14	Is That All There Is?	220
19—20	Is That All There Is?	220
33:11	Is That Your Final Answer?	189
Deuteronomy		
7:1-4	Love is Not Enough	103
7:1-4	Love is Not Enough	105
7:6	Holy Housecleaning	160
12:11	Holy Housecleaning	160
29:29	Is That Your Final Answer?	189
Judges		
21:25	If He Calls You	42
21:25	Who Died and Made You God?	182
1 Samuel		
16:1-13	Is That All There Is?	220
18:12, 14, 28	The Forever House	86

Additional Scripture Passages Referenced

Text	Title	Page
2 Samuel		
3:2-3	Love is Not Enough	103
5:1-5	Inauguration Day	48
5:10	The Forever House	86
7:12	Inauguration Day	48
7:16	Inauguration Day	48
11:2-3	Love is Not Enough	104
11:6-173	Love is Not Enough	104
13:1-223	Love is Not Enough	104
13-23-29	Love is Not Enough	104
13:37-38	Love is Not Enough	104
14:21	Love is Not Enough	105
14:21-24	Love is Not Enough	104
15:2-63	Love is Not Enough	104
18:5, 32	Love is Not Enough	105
23:8, 24, 34, 39	Love is Not Enough	104
1 Kings		
1:32-40	They Could Not Keep Him Out	68
5:2-3	The Forever House	86
9:3	Holy Housecleaning	160
19:11-12	Is That Your Final Answer?	188
21	Is That All There Is?	220
2 Kings		
25:6-7, 27-30	Inauguration Day	48
1 Chronicles		
28:2-3	The Forever House	86
Job		
1:1	The Wisest Thing You'll Ever Do	198
1:21	Blinded by Strength	25
12:23	Holy Housecleaning	160
19:25	Is That Your Final Answer?	191

Additional Scripture Passages Referenced

Text	Title	Page
Psalms		
4:3	Is That You Final Answer?	188
8:1, 9	Is That You Final Answer?	190
22:1	Is That You Final Answer?	190
23:1, 6	The Forever House	89
27:4	In the House of the Lord	136
27:5	In the House of the Lord	137
27:6	In the House of the Lord	137
51:1-4, 7-11	Blinded by Strength	25
100:2, 4	Holy Housecleaning	160
100:3	Who Died and Made You God?	184
119:11	In the House of the Lord	135
122:1	In the House of the Lord	137
Proverbs		
1:7	The Wisest Thing You'll Ever Do	198
26:12	The Wisest Thing You'll Ever Do	198
Isaiah		
6:1	Holy Housecleaning	159
45:18	Who Died and Made You God?	184
53:3	Is That Your Final Answer?	190
53:5	The Forever House	88
53:5-6	Inauguration Day	51
Zechariah		
9:9-10	They Could Not Keep Him Out	70

Additional Scripture Passages Referenced

Text	Title	Page
Matthew		
1:1	Inauguration Day	50
1:18-23	Inauguration Day	51
4:8-10	Lesser Gods—Easier Ways	10
5—7	If He Calls You	40
6:23	If He Calls You	42
6:33	What Shall God Give You	127
7:7	What Shall God Give You	126
7:11	What Shall God Give You	126
7:13	Lesser Gods—Easier Ways	10
7:14	Lesser Gods—Easier Ways	10
8:1-3	Holy Housecleaning	153
10:39	Lesser Gods—Easier Ways	10
15:30-31	They Could Not Keep Him Out	70
16:24	The Forever House	86
18:13	Inauguration Day	49
18:20	In the House of the Lord	134
21:8-9	They Could Not Keep Him Out	68
21:12-13	They Could Not Keep Him Out	69
23:1-3	Inauguration Day	49
25:31-33	Who Died and Made You God?	185
26:3-5	They Could Not Keep Him Out	69
27:41-43	They Could Not Keep Him Out	69
27:45	Hope in the Darkness	99
27:46	Is That Your Final Answer?	190
27:57-60	Is That All There Is?	221
Mark		
8:1-12	Prove It!	16
10:46-52	They Could Not Keep Him Out	67
11:8-9	They Could Not Keep Him Out	68
11:11	They Could Not Keep Him Out	69
14:55-59	They Could Not Keep Him Out	70
15:25, 33-37	They Could Not Keep Him Out	70

Additional Scripture Passages Referenced

Text	Title	Page
Luke		
1:26-31	Inauguration Day	50
1:26-35	Inauguration Day	51
2:8-11	A Word To (and From) the Wise	203
2:8-12	Inauguration Day	51
2:22-38	Inauguration Day	51
2:42-47	Inauguration Day	51
9:23	Lesser Gods—Easier Ways	10
17:11-19	Holy Housecleaning	153
19:37-38	They Could Not Keep Him Out	68
19:47-48	They Could Not Keep Him Out	69
22:24-27	Blinded by Strength	25
23:34	Hope in the Darkness	99
John		
1:14	Holy Housecleaning	163
1:14	A Word To (and From) the Wise	203
1:18	Who Died and Made You God?	184
2:19	The Forever House	89
2:19	In the House of the Lord	131
3:8	Blinded by Strength	25
3:16	Inauguration Day	50
3:16	The Forever House	88
3:16	A Word To (and From) the Wise	203
4:42	Inauguration Day	51
6:38	What Shall God Give You	126
10:2-3, 14-16	If He Calls You	44
10:10	Inauguration Day	52
10:10	Is That Your Final Answer?	191
11:38-44	They Could Not Keep Him Out	67
12:23, 25, 27	For Such a Time as This	173
13:5-14	The Forever House	88
14:6	Lesser Gods—Easier Ways	10
14:16-17	What Shall God Give You	126
15:7	What Shall God Give You	124
16:23	What Shall God Give You	124

Additional Scripture Passages Referenced

Text	Title	Page

John (Continued)

19	Is That All There Is?	221
19:1	The Forever House	88
19:1-3	They Could Not Keep Him Out	70
19:12-16	They Could Not Keep Him Out	70
19:16-18	They Could Not Keep Him Out	69
20:1-16	Is That All There Is?	221
20:19	They Could Not Keep Him Out	70
20:19-31	Is That Your Final Answer?	191
20:24-25	Is That Your Final Answer?	191
20:27	Is That Your Final Answer?	192
20:28	Is That Your Final Answer?	192

Acts

2:21	Inauguration Day	52
16:31	Inauguration Day	52

Romans

1:19-22	Who Died and Made You God?	183
1:22	Who Died and Made You God?	184
3:10, 23	Inauguration Day	51
5:2b-5	Hope in the Darkness	98
5:5	Hope in the Darkness	99
5:9-10	Inauguration Day	52
8:11	Love is Not Enough	109
8:28	For Such a Time as This	171
12:5-6	Blinded by Strength	24
14:8-9	For Such a Time as This	173

1 Corinthians

2:2	Is That Your Final Answer?	192
6:19	If He Calls You	41
11:23-26	If He Calls You	40

Additional Scripture Passages Referenced

Text	Title	Page
2 Corinthians		
4:8-9	Hope in the Darkness	97
5:17-19	Inauguration Day	52
5:21	Inauguration Day	50
5:21	The Forever House	88
6:14	Love Is Not Enough	105
12:9	Blinded by Strength	25
Ephesians		
2:22	In the House of the Lord	134
2:21-22	In the House of the Lord	135
3:16-19	Things That Kings Can't Do	154
3:20-21	What Shall God Give You?	127
6:4	Is That Your Final Answer?	189
Philippians		
2:5-8	Love is Not Enough	108
2:6-7	They Could Not Keep Him Out	69
2:10-11	They Could Not Keep Him Out	72
2:10-11	Inauguration Day	49
Colossians		
1:15-16	Inauguration Day	48
1:19	Things That Kings Can't Do	154
1 Timothy		
6:5	Inauguration Day	48
Titus		
3:5	Inauguration Day	52
Hebrews		
2:14-15	Inauguration Day	51
4:15	Inauguration Day	50
7:11	The Forever House	88
9:27	Who Died and Made You God?	185

Additional Scripture Passages Referenced

Text	Title	Page
James		
1:22	Who Died and Made You God?	185
4:3	What Shall God Give You	124
1 Peter		
1:20-21	Love is Not Enough	109
2:24	The Forever House	88
5:4	Who Died and Made You God?	185
1 John		
2:2	The Forever House	88
4:1	Prove It!	16
4:9	For Such a Time as This	174
4:9-10	Love is Not Enough	108
4:14	Inauguration Day	51
Revelation		
1:18	Who Died and Made You God?	185
3:20	Inauguration Day	51
3:20	They Could Not Keep Him Out	71
3:21	They Could Not Keep Him Out	73
4:8	Who Died and Made You God?	184
11:15	Inauguration Day	48
11:15	They Could Not Keep Him Out	72
11:15	The Forever House	89
17:14	Inauguration Day	48
19:16	Inauguration Day	48
20:4	Who Died and Made You God?	185
21:1	A Word To (and From) the Wise	203
21:1-6	Is That All There Is?	221
22:5	Inauguration Day	48

Related Sermons in Other Volumes

Text	Title	Page (in Other Volumes)

In *Walking with Jesus*

1 Samuel
16:11-13   Inauguration Day 5

In *Not Exactly What They Expected*

2 Samuel
5:1-3, 6-7   They Could Not Keep Him Out 15
15:13-30   Hope in the Darkness 75

www.ingramcontent.com/pod-product-compliance
Lightning Source LLC
Chambersburg PA
CBHW020849090426
42736CB00008B/306